French 2

*Foundation Skills
for 11-14 year olds*

Gloria Richards BA

Head of French,
Senior Tutor to the Sixth Form,
Brynteg Comprehensive School

Charles Letts & Co Ltd
London, Edinburgh & New York

First published 1986
by Charles Letts & Co Ltd
Diary House, Borough Road, London SE1 1DW

Illustrations: Kate Charlesworth, Chartwell Illustrators

ISBN 0 85097 660 X

Printed in Great Britain by
Charles Letts (Scotland) Ltd

Acknowledgements
I wish to express my thanks to the following people for
their help in producing this book:

Ian Bryden who acted as consultant, for his wise counsel
and professional advice; Mlle Marie-Jeanne Zitoune and
Mrs J. M. Dennis for their revision of the manuscript; Guy
Droz, Samuel Blythe Farnsworth and Vaughan Richards
for the photographs; Pat Rowlinson, Anne Henwood and
the staff of Letts for their guidance and expertise; and
above all my husband and daughter for their unfailing
support and encouragement.

Preface

This book has been written as a study aid for pupils in their second year of learning French. Pupils often find learning a foreign language difficult in the early years when faced with the demands of acquiring new skills in listening, speaking, reading and writing in French. This book, like Volume 1, aims to help pupils assimilate and practise the core elements of those French courses which are used in schools today. Some courses are based on graded schemes of work whereas others are based on more traditional lines. This book may be used by pupils following both traditional and modern courses.

The emphasis is on the practical application of knowledge and the reader is encouraged throughout to use his/her knowledge actively in communication. Each Unit has as its focal point an everyday situation or situations with sufficient vocabulary and grammatical explanation to provide a sound basis for participation in that particular situation. The acquisition of grammatical knowledge is a necessary part of this study aid and without it the perfection of skills is impossible. The reader is encouraged to listen, speak, read and write in French with confidence and above all to involve himself/herself in the active use of French.

Gloria D. Richards
1986

4

Contents

Introduction

and guide to using this book

This Foundation series aims to help pupils acquire the knowledge and skills which are necessary for success in learning French. The acquisition of such knowledge and skills requires careful learning and then plenty of practice. As in Volume 1, each Unit in this book contains essential information, grammatical explanation and practice 'Activités' which have been devised to help pupils acquire and improve their listening, speaking, reading and writing skills in French.

Approach

You should work systematically through this book learning all the new words, grammar and then do all the Activités in the order given. When you have finished each Unit, check your answers in the Answer Section.

Method

1 Listening skills

Although it is difficult to practise this skill from a book, there are several ways in which you can gain extra practice.

(a) Always listen to your teacher in class carefully and try to imitate the sounds you hear as closely as possible when it is your turn to speak in French.

(b) Listen to French Radio as often as you can. (French Radio stations can be received on most sets in the British Isles.) You may not be able to understand all that is being said on French Radio but listen carefully to the way in which sounds are produced.

(c) Watch as many French language programmes on TV as possible. Begin with the simpler level programmes to gain confidence and then progress to the more difficult ones. Always try to imitate the sounds you hear.

(d) In some of the Units, you will find Activités where you are told that someone is speaking in French and you are asked to explain in English what is being said. Ask a French native speaker or your teacher to record these Activités on tape for you so that you can listen to an actual voice when practising.

2 Speaking skills

The advice given to you in 'listening skills' also applies to 'speaking skills'. Always try to imitate the sounds you hear from native speakers.

In many of the Activités in this book you are asked to 'say in French. . . '. Always check with your teacher if you are not sure of a sound. Here are some general pointers to help you with your pronunciation.

(a) The letter 'h' is never pronounced in French when it is the first letter of the word.

(b) As a general rule a final consonant is pronounced only if the next word begins with a vowel.

e.g. dans la maison (the 's' in 'dans' is *not* pronounced)
dan*s* une maison (the 's' in 'dans' *is* pronounced)

(c) The end of the word is usually emphasized in French, unlike English.

e.g. English: Im*pos*sible
French : Imposs*ible*

English: In*tell*igent
French : Intellig*ent*

(d) There are lots of nasal sounds in French. Try holding your nose and saying 'un'. This is the sound you need to make in French but without actually holding your nose!

(e) The French 'r' is produced in a different way from the English 'r'. In French it should be produced at the back of the throat. Here is an exercise to help you to practise this (do not over-practise this at first, however, as you may give yourself a sore throat):

Open the mouth wide and say 'ah'. Keep the mouth in this open position and say 'ah-ara-ra'. The rolling of the 'r' at the back of the throat should now be clearly heard.

(f) The 'u' sound in French (heard in such words as 'du' 'vu' 'vend*u*', etc.) is another sound which, if pronounced correctly, will make your spoken words sound more 'French'. Practise the following exercise to help you to improve this sound:

Push the lips out into a tight 'O' shape and say 'oo'. (This sound should be the same as in the word 'too' but without the 't'.)

Now stretch your lips wide and say 'ee' (as in 'tee').

To produce a perfect French 'u' sound, you should now try to say 'ee' in the 'oo' mouth position. Remember not to move your lips from the 'oo' position when trying to say 'ee'.

3 Reading skills

Always read carefully. Never 'skip' sentences. Each word is important and spelling is very important. You only know a language really well when you can read and write (i.e. spell) it correctly, as well as speak it and understand the spoken word.

Before answering any questions on a reading passage, make sure that you have really understood the passage. Be prepared to read a passage several times, if necessary, before attempting to answer the questions on the passage.

If you are translating, remember that the English you write is as important as the French you are reading. Never write a stilted translation which looks as if it has obviously been translated. Always use the most natural, but correct, expressions from each language.

4 Writing skills

There are many writing exercises for you to do in this book. Remember that not only is correct spelling important but that accents, too, must be written correctly. When you learn the spelling of a word, learn the correct accent too, if there is one. At the end of each written Activité always check carefully what you have written before going on to the next section. The good habits you form now will be invaluable to you in the later stages of language learning.

Some of the written Activités will be preparing you for 'free composition' work which you will have to do later when preparing for public examinations in French. The keys to success in this type of question are simplicity and, above all, accuracy. If you take care to check your work now, in the early stages of language learning, you will reap many benefits later.

All of the above skills are tested in schools in some form or other. Many schools now use Graded Tests to assess the progress of pupils. Many of the Activités in this book are similar to the ones you may have to do in your Graded Assessment tests or APU (Assessment of Performance Unit) tests. *Foundation Skills French* will help you to gain confidence and not to panic when taking these tests. By carefully and consistently working through this book, you will have a firm base for future work in French in school. Set aside a specific day(s) and time each week for using this book, and keep to it!

Vocabulary

Essential vocabulary and key words are given in each Unit. Learn all new words as you meet them. Before proceeding to a new Unit, make sure that you really do know all the new words from the present Unit.

Grammar

This has been reduced to a necessary minimum but is nevertheless important. Learn each new 'rule' as you meet it and, above all, remember it. Imagine that you are working with building blocks. You must not leave any gaps or else your basic skills will be in danger of collapsing.

Activités

There are many different Activités in this book which will give you lots of practice for Graded Tests. Here are some of the different things you will be asked to do:
reading comprehension;
listening comprehension;
answering questions about yourself and others;
completion exercises;
role-play;
interpreting;
asking questions;
giving directions;
understanding directions;
giving commands;
expressing likes and dislikes;
ordering things;
shopping;
going through Customs;
dealing with officials;
writing letters.

Unit 1

Les vacances/
Holidays

In this unit you will:
(1) revise some important verbs from Volume 1;
(2) learn the verb 'devoir' (to have to/to owe);
(3) learn how to use the pronoun 'on' (one);
(4) practise giving directions in French.

La famille Gavarin à Londres

La famille Gavarin est en vacances en Angleterre. Ils sont à Londres. C'est leur première visite en Grande-Bretagne. Ils vont visiter tous les monuments historiques à Londres, mais Madame Gavarin et Céline ont l'intention d'aller aux magasins aussi. Monsieur Gavarin n'aime pas les magasins et il dit qu'on y dépense trop d'argent. Il préfère les musées. Madame Gavarin dit à son mari que les vêtements sont moins chers à Londres et qu'on doit profiter des vacances pour acheter des robes d'hiver pour elle et pour Céline.

D'abord la famille Gavarin va au Syndicat d'Initiative. Là on donne à la famille tous les renseignements sur la ville. On explique où trouver un bon hôtel, comment voyager en métro, comment commander des billets de théâtre, etc. En été il y a tellement de monde à Londres – des touristes anglais et surtout des touristes étrangers – que les accents sont multiples et on a quelquefois des difficultés à se comprendre.

Les Gavarin cherchent un hôtel près des grands magasins. Ils ont un plan de la ville qui est bien utile car on peut se perdre facilement dans une ville inconnue. Il fait beau mais pas trop chaud à Londres en été. La famille Gavarin est bien contente d'être en vacances.

Devoir

Here is another irregular verb which you will frequently need to use.

devoir to have to
to owe

je dois	I have to, I must, I owe,
tu dois	etc.
il doit	
elle doit	
nous devons	
vous devez	
ils doivent	
elles doivent	

The pronoun 'on'

You will frequently hear French people using the word 'on' in a sentence instead of 'je/nous/ils/elles, etc.'. It is used in a general sense to mean 'one/someone/people, etc.'. 'On' always takes the 'il'/'elle' part of the verb. Here are some examples from the passage at the beginning of this Unit.

On y dépense trop d'argent.
(*One* spends too much money there.)
or You spend too much money there.
or We spend too much money there.
On doit profiter des vacances pour acheter des robes d'hiver.
(*One/we* must take advantage of the holidays to buy winter dresses.)

On donne à la famille tous les renseignements sur la ville.
(*One* gives/*they* give the family all the information about the town.)

On peut se perdre facilement dans une ville inconnue.
(*One/you* can easily get lost in a strange town.)

Here are some more sentences using 'on' which you might hear in France. Each one tells you about a different kind of holiday.
(a) On va passer les vacances à l'étranger.
(b) On va passer les vacances chez soi.
(c) On passe les vacances chez des parents.
(d) On passe les vacances au bord de la mer.
(e) On voyage en Europe.
(f) On reste à la campagne.
(g) On va rester à l'hôtel.
(h) On va louer une villa.
(i) On cherche une villa sur la Côte d'Azur.
(j) On fait du camping.

New words
passer to spend (time)
à l'étranger abroad
chez soi at (one's) home
les parents parents/relatives
louer to hire/rent
une villa villa/house
la Côte d'Azur the Riviera

Activités

1 Read the passage aloud in French and learn
   the new words.

New words

anglais English
l'Angleterre (*f*) England
avoir l'intention de to intend
car for, because
(se) comprendre to understand (each other)
commander to order
comment how
dépenser to spend
la difficulté difficulty
elle (also) her
un étranger stranger/foreigner
expliquer to explain
facilement easily
la Grande-Bretagne Great Britain
inconnu(e) unknown/strange
Londres London
le métro underground railway
le monument historique historic monument
multiple many
le musée museum
on doit one must
on peut one can
(se) perdre to lose (oneself)
profiter de to take advantage of
que* that
qui* which
les renseignements (*m*) information
surtout especially
tellement de monde such a lot of people
trouver to find
utile useful
en vacances on holiday
voyager to travel

* **You will learn more about these in Unit 2.**

2 Answer the following questions by choosing
   which answer you think is the most suitable.

(a) How many times has the Gavarin family
    already been to England before this visit?
     (i) 0
     (ii) 1
     (iii) 2
     (iv) 3

(b) What is every member of the Gavarin family
    going to do while in London?
     (i) Go shopping
     (ii) Spend money
     (iii) Go sightseeing
     (iv) Only go to museums

(c) What do Mrs Gavarin and Céline especially
    want to do?
     (i) Stay in a hotel
     (ii) Go shopping
     (iii) Go to the museums
     (iv) Go to the Tourist Information Office

(d) What does Mr Gavarin want to do?
     (i) Go with Mrs Gavarin and Céline
     (ii) Spend his money
     (iii) Go to the Tourist Information Office
     (iv) Go to the museums

(e) What does Mrs Gavarin think about the
    clothes in English shops?
     (i) They are less expensive than in France
     (ii) They are more expensive than in France
     (iii) They are more attractive than in France
     (iv) They are less attractive than in France

(f) What does Mrs Gavarin wish to buy?
     (i) A summer dress for herself
     (ii) A summer dress for Céline
     (iii) A winter dress for herself
     (iv) A winter dress for herself and Céline

(g) At the Tourist Information Office, the Gavarin
    family is given . . .
     (i) all kinds of information
     (ii) information about the weather
     (iii) information about the foreign tourists in
          London
     (iv) information about the accents in London

(h) The Gavarins are looking for a hotel . . .
     (i) where there are other foreign tourists
     (ii) where there are English tourists
     (iii) near to the shops
     (iv) away from the shops

(i) Why do people find it difficult to understand
    each other in London?
     (i) There are so many people there
     (ii) There are so many different accents
     (iii) There are too many tourists
     (iv) The guide is difficult to understand

(j) What is the weather usually like in London in
    summer according to the passage?
     (i) Cold
     (ii) Fine
     (iii) Too hot
     (iv) Wet

3 Can you remember all the different parts of
   these verbs which you learnt in Volume 1?

aller, avoir, être, faire

Complete the following sentences with the correct
part of the verb.

(a) Elle (faire) des achats.
(b) Nous (être) à Londres.
(c) Tu (avoir) un bon accent.
(d) Ils (aller) au Syndicat d'Initiative.
(e) Je (aller) visiter les monuments historiques.
(f) Vous (faire) une promenade.

(g) Elles (avoir) l'intention d'aller aux magasins.
(h) Je (être) en vacances.
(i) Il (faire) beau.
(j) Vous (être) devant l'hôtel.

4 Learn carefully all the parts of the verb 'devoir'.

5 Complete the following sentences with the correct part of the verb.

(a) Nous d..... faire des achats.
(b) Je d... chercher un hôtel.
(c) Vous d.... aller au Syndicat d'Initiative.
(d) Tu d... visiter les monuments historiques.
(e) Elles d...... acheter des robes d'hiver.
(f) Il d... aller au musée.
(g) Nous d..... regarder le plan de la ville.
(h) Ils d...... voyager à Londres.
(i) Je d... partir de bonne heure.
(j) Elle d... chercher un hôtel.

6 Now say what the sentences mean in English.

7 Learn the new words.

8 Here are some English sentences which are the equivalent of the French sentences on page 9 but in the wrong order. Rearrange the French sentences by writing them in your Record Book in the same order as the following English sentences.

(a) We are looking for a house on the Riviera.
(b) They are travelling in Europe.
(c) They are staying in the country.
(d) We are going to spend the holidays abroad.
(e) They are camping.
(f) They are going to stay in a hotel.
(g) We are spending the holidays by the sea.
(h) We are going to spend the holidays at home.
(i) We are spending the holidays with relatives.
(j) We are going to rent a villa.

9 Now read aloud the sentences you have written in your Record Book in French.

10 Do you remember the different ways of giving directions which you learnt in Volume 1? Check back to Volume 1 if you are unsure before attempting this Activité.

Here is part of a map of London. You have met a French family on holiday in London and are helping them by giving them the following directions in French. What would you say to them in French to direct them from . . .

(a) A (Buckingham Palace) to B (Trafalgar Square)?
(b) B (Trafalgar Square) to C (The Embankment)?
(c) C (The Embankment) to D (The Houses of Parliament)*?
(d) D (The Houses of Parliament) to E (Westminster Abbey)?

* **Les Palais du Parlement**.

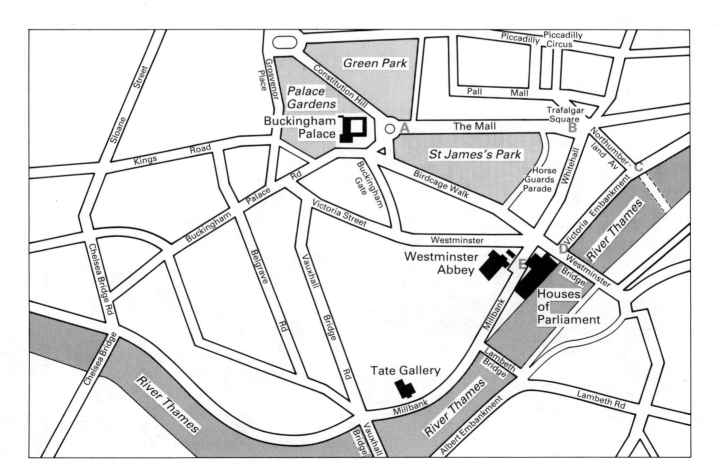

Unit 2

Au camping/ Camping

In this unit you will learn:
(1) some useful vocabulary for camping in France;
(2) how to seek information about camping in France;
(3) how to book a campsite in France;
(4) the relative pronouns 'qui' and 'que'.

New words

le bâtiment sanitaire
le bloc sanitaire } washrooms/toilets
le bureau d'acceuil   reception
le bureau de renseignements   information
   office
le camping   campsite
la canne à pêche   fishing-rod
la caravane   caravan
faire du camping   to go camping
la chaise pliante   folding-chair
les douches (*f*)   showers
un emplacement   pitch/site
les lavabos   washrooms
les poubelles (*f*)   dustbins
la salle de jeux   games room
le réchaud   camping-stove
le sac de couchage   sleeping-bag
la piscine   swimming-pool
la table pliante   folding-table
la tente   tent
le terrain de camping   campsite

Learn the following new words before reading the passage.

pendant que   while
une année   year
après   after(wards)
attraper   to catch
la cantine   canteen
couler   to flow
délicieux   delicious
le français   French
herbeux   grassy
la journée   day
naturellement   naturally
ombragé   shady/shaded
parce qu(e)   because
(en) plein air   (in) the open air
parler   to speak
le repas   meal
tranquille   quiet
la tranquillité   tranquillity
se trouver   to be found

La famille Latille au camping

Pendant que la famille Gavarin est en vacances à Londres, leurs cousins Latille sont en vacances en France. Monsieur et Madame Latille préfèrent la France parce qu'en France on parle français . . .

naturellement et aussi parce qu'il fait toujours beau en été. La famille Latille aime faire du camping. Cette année ils choisissent un camping qui est bien tranquille à huit kilomètres de Villeneuve-sur-Yonne. Là le terrain de camping est herbeux et ombragé. Les Latille aiment bien la tranquillité de leur emplacement qui se trouve au bord de la rivière. Les enfants qui sont très contents vont à la pêche. Ils attrapent beaucoup de poissons que la famille mange au repas du soir.

'Le poisson que nous mangeons* ce soir est délicieux,' dit Madame Latille.

'Moi, je préfère le poisson que nous mangeons à la maison,' dit Marie-Jeanne, 'mais je déteste le poisson qu'on mange à la cantine de l'école.'

Après le repas du soir qu'on mange devant la tente, la famille fait une promenade au bord de la rivière qui coule près du camping. Les enfants sont très fatigués après une journée en plein air.

*   **In the 'nous' form of the verb 'manger' the 'e' is retained.**

The relative pronouns 'qui' and 'que' ('qu'')

In the passage above you can see several examples of sentences using 'qui'/'que'/'qu'' to link two ideas together.

'Qui'

(a) Ils choisissent un camping **qui** est bien tranquille.

The two ideas in this sentence are . . .
   (1) They choose a campsite.
   (2) The campsite is quiet.

The word 'qui' (which) is used as a linking word, and is the *subject* of the verb 'est'.

(b) Les enfants **qui** sont très contents vont à la pêche.

The two ideas in this sentence are . . .
   (1) The children are happy.
   (2) They are going fishing.

The word 'qui' (who) is the *subject* of 'sont'. Therefore, 'qui' has two meanings: (i) who, (ii) which. It is always the *subject* of the verb which follows.

'Que' ('qu'')

Look at these examples from the passage you have just read.

Le poisson **que** nous mangeons ce soir est délicieux.
Après le repas du soir **qu'on** mange devant la tente . . .

In these two sentences the link word 'que' ('qu'') is the *object* of the verb which follows.
'Que' is changed to **'qu''** before a vowel.

14

Activités

1 Learn all the new words on page 13.

2 Without looking at the new words, answer the following in French.

Qu'est-ce que c'est?
Use **C'est mon** . . .
or **C'est ma** . . .   in the answers.

e.g.

C'est ma caravane.

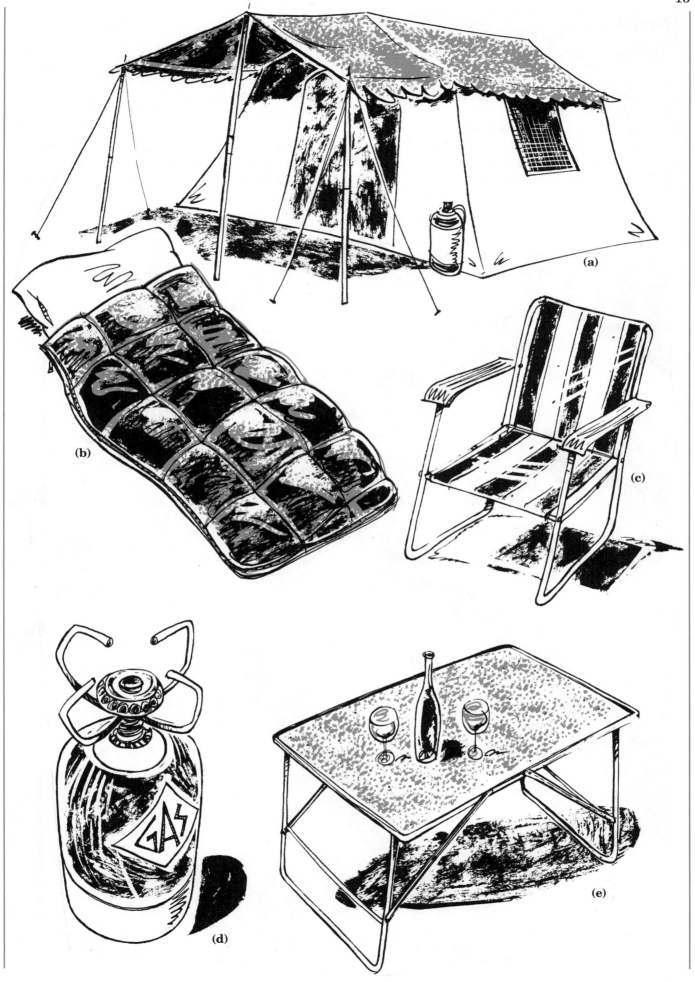

Activités *continued*

3 You are staying at a campsite in France. You are unable to find the following. How would you ask in French . . .?

e.g. Where are the caravans please?
      Où sont les caravanes, s'il vous plaît?

(a) Where are the showers, please?
(b) Where are the toilets, please?
(c) Where is* the swimming-pool, please?
(d) Where is the reception, please?
(e) Where are the dustbins, please?
(f) Where is the games room, please?
(g) Where is the information office, please?
(h) Where are the caravans, please?
(i) Where is my sleeping-bag?
(j) Where are the washrooms/toilets, please?**

*   **Remember to use a singular verb here.**
** **The noun you need in this sentence is singular. Remember to use a singular verb here.**

4 Read the passage aloud in French, then answer the questions by choosing which answer you think is the most appropriate.

(a) Where are the Latilles taking their holiday?
  (i) abroad
  (ii) in their own country
  (iii) in London
  (iv) with their cousins

(b) What is one of the reasons for their choice?
  (i) The weather is always fine.
  (ii) They don't have to speak French.
  (iii) They love nature.
  (iv) It is less expensive.

(c) How far is the campsite from Villeneuve-sur-Yonne?
  (i) 8 kilomètres
  (ii) 18 kilomètres
  (iii) 28 kilomètres
  (iv) 80 kilomètres

(d) The campsite is . . .
  (i) noisy
  (ii) near a town
  (iii) quiet
  (iv) well-equipped

(e) Why are the children pleased about their pitch?
  (i) It is near their friends.
  (ii) It is near the river.
  (iii) It is near the restaurant.
  (iv) It is near the swimming-pool.

(f) What do the family eat for their evening meal?
  (i) fish
  (ii) meat
  (iii) peaches
  (iv) chips

(g) What does Marie-Jeanne prefer eating?
  (i) fish at home
  (ii) fish at school
  (iii) fish in the canteen
  (iv) fish at the campsite

(h) Where does the family have its evening meal?
  (i) in the tent
  (ii) in front of the tent
  (iii) by the side of the tent
  (iv) in the restaurant

(i) What do the family do after their evening meal?
  (i) go to bed
  (ii) walk on the promenade
  (iii) go on the river
  (iv) go for a walk

(j) Why are the children tired?
  (i) They've had a full day.
  (ii) They've eaten too much.
  (iii) They got up very early.
  (iv) They've had a lot of fresh air.

5 Link each pair of sentences given below with the word 'qui'.
e.g.   Voilà les enfants. Ils* jouent devant la tente.
   Voilà les enfants **qui** jouent devant la tente.

* **N.B. 'Qui' is used *instead* of this word.**

(a) Voilà les enfants. Ils jouent derrière la tente.
(b) Voilà le terrain de camping. Il est au bord de la rivière.
(c) Regardez ces enfants. Ils pêchent dans la rivière.
(d) Je préfère notre emplacement. Il est ombragé.
(e) Nous allons faire une promenade au bord de la rivière. Elle coule près du camping.

6 Now say what the completed sentences mean in English.

7 Link each pair of sentences given below with 'que' or 'qu'' (before a vowel).
e.g.   C'est un camping ombragé. Nous cherchons *un camping ombragé.**

* **As these words are given in the first sentence they are omitted in the 'linked' sentence . . .**

   C'est un camping ombragé **que** nous cherchons.

(a) C'est un terrain de camping ombragé. Nous cherchons un terrain de camping ombragé.
(b) C'est un terrain de camping herbeux. Nous cherchons un terrain de camping herbeux.
(c) C'est un terrain de camping herbeux. On cherche un terrain de camping herbeux.
(d) Voilà le camping. Nous cherchons le camping.
(e) Voici la caravane. On cherche la caravane.

8 Now say what the completed sentences mean in English.

9 Answer the following questions about yourself in French. If your answers to questions **(c)**, **(d)**, **(e)** are negative, use **de** instead of **un/une**.

(a) Aimes-tu faire du camping?
(b) Préfères-tu faire du camping ou rester à l'hôtel?
(c) As-tu une tente?
(d) As-tu une caravane?
(e) As-tu un sac de couchage?

10 You are seeking information about a campsite in France. What would you say in French to ask for the following information?
e.g.   Is the campsite near a river?
   (Le camping est près d'une rivière?)

(a) Is the campsite quiet?
(b) Is the campsite shaded?
(c) Is there a swimming-pool?
(d) Is there a restaurant?
(e) Is the campsite near the town?

Unit 3

A l'hôtel/
At the hotel

In this unit you will learn:
(1) the adjective 'tout' (all/every);
(2) more about 'er' verbs;
(3) how to book a hotel room in France;
(4) how to check your hotel bill.

'Tout'

The adjective 'tout' which means 'all' or 'every' has four different forms in French . . .

masc. sing. 'tout'   e.g. **tout** le monde
                                   (everybody)
fem. sing.   'toute'   e.g. **toute** la famille
                                   (all the family)
masc. pl.   'tous'   e.g. **tous** les repas
                                   (all the meals)
fem. pl.   'toutes' e.g. **toutes** les chambres
                                   (all the rooms)

Sometimes the word 'tout' is used without a noun. In this case it means 'everything'.

In the following passage you will see examples of the different forms of 'tout'.

HOTEL DE BRETAGNE

BAR·RESTAURANT   HOTEL DE BRETAGNE

Dans un hôtel

Tout le monde aime rester dans un hôtel. Il y a tout pour votre confort. Tous les repas sont préparés pour vous. Tous les matins on fait votre lit. On est bien content de rester dans un hôtel. Si vous le désirez, on vous appelle le matin. Mais si vous préférez rester au lit, on vous laisse tranquille. D'habitude on peut prendre le petit déjeuner dans la chambre ou dans la salle à manger. Les parents et les enfants sont contents à l'hôtel. Si les enfants jettent toutes leurs affaires par terre, la femme de ménage qui range les chambres tous les jours va les ramasser. Mais si les enfants sont gentils, ils disent à leurs parents 'Nous rangeons nos affaires nous-mêmes'.

New words

le confort   comfort
préparé(s)   prepared
laisser   to leave
d'habitude   usually
jettent   throw (the verb 'jeter' appears later in this Unit)
toutes leurs affaires   all their belongings
par terre   on the ground
la femme de ménage   the maid
ranger   to tidy/clear up
ramasser   to pick up
gentil   nice/kind
nous-mêmes   ourselves

'–er' verbs

Can you remember the different endings to '–er' verbs which you learnt in Volume 1?

Here is a reminder for you.

Regular '–er' verbs

e.g.   **rester**   (to stay)

je	–e	**je reste** I stay
tu	–es	**tu restes** you (*singular*) stay
il	–e	**il reste** he stays
elle	–e	**elle reste** she stays
nous	–ons	**nous restons** we stay
vous	–ez	**vous restez** you (*plural and polite singular*) stay
ils	–ent	**ils restent** they (*masc.*) stay
elles	–ent	**elles restent** they (*fem.*) stay

Changes to '–er' verbs

(a) In Unit 2 and in this Unit you have seen the 'nous' form of the verbs **manger** (to eat) and **ranger** (to tidy up). The 'nous' form of these verbs retains the 'e' after the 'g' in order to soften the letter 'g'.

nous **mangeons** (we eat)
nous **rangeons** (we tidy up)

(b) The verb **commencer** is another verb which has an addition to the 'nous' form of the verb. In this case it is a cedilla (¸):

nous **commençons** (we begin)

(c) Other verbs have more changes. The verbs **jeter** (to throw) and **appeler** (to call) have the following changes:

jeter	appeler
je jette I throw,	j'appelle I call,
tu jettes etc.	tu appelles etc.
il jette	il appelle
elle jette	elle appelle
nous jetons*	nous appelons*
vous jetez*	vous appelez*
ils jettent	ils appellent
elles jettent	elles appellent

*   **N.B. the single consonant in these forms (i.e. 't' and 'l') *but* double consonants in the others.**

(d) At the end of Volume 1 you learnt the verb **préférer**, with the accent changes which occur in the present tense in all parts except the 'nous'/'vous' forms. Here is another verb with the same accent changes:

répéter   (to repeat)
je répète   I repeat,

tu répètes   etc.
il répète
elle répète
nous répétons
vous répétez
ils répètent
elles répètent

Unit 3 continued

The verb **espérer** (to hope) has only one accent. This accent changes in the same way.

espérer
j'espère I hope,
tu espères etc.
il espère
elle espère
nous espérons
vous espérez
ils espèrent
elles espèrent

(e) Finally, verbs which end in '–oyer' e.g. **envoyer** (to send) have a letter change in all parts except the 'nous'/'vous' forms.

envoyer
j'envoie I send,
tu envoies etc.
il envoie
elle envoie
nous envoyons
vous envoyez
ils envoient
elles envoient

N.B. An easy way to remember all of these verb changes is to remember that the 'nous/'vous' forms are like the infinitives and that it is the other parts which change.

A la réception de l'hôtel

Touriste: Bonjour, monsieur, avez-vous des chambres libres?
Propriétaire: Combien de chambres désirez-vous?
Touriste: Deux chambres à deux lits, s'il vous plaît.
Propriétaire: Avec ou sans salle de bain?
Touriste: Une chambre avec salle de bain et l'autre avec douche, s'il vous plaît.
Propriétaire: C'est pour combien de nuits, monsieur?
Touriste: Pour trois nuits.
Propriétaire: Alors, nous avons une chambre à deux lits avec salle de bain au premier étage et une chambre avec douche au troisième étage.
Touriste: Y a-t-il un ascenseur?
Propriétaire: Oui, monsieur.
Touriste: Quel est le prix des chambres?
Propriétaire: La chambre au premier étage est à cent douze francs la nuit et la chambre au troisième étage est à quatre-vingt-dix francs la nuit. Le petit déjeuner n'est pas compris.
Touriste: Je voudrais voir les chambres.

New words

la réception reception (desk)
libre free
le (la) propriétaire owner
une chambre à deux lits double room
(**une chambre à un lit** single room)
sans without
l'étage storey/floor
un ascenseur lift

A French hotel bill

Here is a bill for three people staying in a hotel in Paris for four nights. The room (given here as 'appartement') costs 196 francs per night. The breakfast costs 10 francs for each of the three people. The total at the bottom of each column is placed at the top of the next column on the line 'report' (carried forward). At the bottom of the bill in writing are the words. 'lit supp.' ('lit supplémentaire' means an extra bed). An extra bed was included in the room for the third person (a child). The extra bed costs 74 francs per night.
× IIII – for four nights.
'Débours du concierge' means 'extras'.

If you are lucky enough to stay in a hotel in France, look carefully at the bill (**a**) to check that it is correct and (**b**) to see if there are any new words to learn.

Activités

1 Read the passage aloud in French and learn all the new words.

2 Answer the following questions about the passage in English.

(a) Give two reasons why it is said people like staying in hotels.
(b) In what two places can you usually have breakfast?
(c) What other optional service is provided in the mornings?
(d) How often does the maid tidy up the rooms?
(e) At the end of the passage what do the children tell their parents?

3 Give the verb its correct form in the following sentences.

(a) Tu (jeter) tes affaires par terre.
(b) Nous (ranger) nos affaires.
(c) J' (appeler) la femme de ménage.
(d) Ils (appeler) la femme de ménage.
(e) Nous (commencer) le petit déjeuner.
(f) Elle (envoyer) une carte postale à ses amis.
(g) Je (répéter) la question.
(h) Il (espérer) arriver ce soir.
(i) Vous (espérer) rester à l'hôtel?
(j) Elles (commencer) leurs vacances.

4 Now say what the completed sentences mean in English.

5 Read the passage and learn all the new words.

6 Answer the following questions in English.
(a) How many rooms is the tourist looking for?
(b) Are they single or double rooms?
(c) Does he want them with or without a bathroom?
(d) How many nights are they going to stay?
(e) Is there a lift in the hotel?
(f) On which floor is the double room with a shower?
(g) What is the cost per night of this room?
(h) On which floor is the double room with a bathroom?
(i) What is the cost per night of this room?
(j) Is breakfast included in the cost of the room?

7 You are at the reception desk of a hotel. What would you say in French to ask for the following?

(a) Do you have a double room with bathroom please?
(b) Do you have a double room without a bathroom please?
(c) Do you have a double room with a shower please?
(d) Do you have a single room on the first floor please?
(e) Do you have a double room on the first floor please?
(f) Is there a lift?
(g) How much does the room cost?
(h) Is breakfast included?

8 Look at the hotel bill, answer the following questions.

(a) Is the final total correct on this bill?
(b) What does the bill come to
  (i) in francs?
  (ii) in £ sterling at 11.30f to the £?

Unit 4

La routine journalière/ Daily routine

In this unit you will:
(1) learn about reflexive verbs;
(2) learn the verb 'mettre' (to put (on));
(3) revise 'time'.

Reflexive verbs

Under the pictures on this page you can see three verbs (infinitives) which tell us what is happening in each picture. They are all '–er' verbs but they have 'se' placed in front. These are called 'reflexive' verbs. The endings of the different parts are the same as other regular '–er' verbs but the 'se' will change during the verb. Reflexive verbs always refer to an action done to 'self'.

e.g. **se laver** to get washed/to wash oneself

je **me** lave I get washed/I wash myself,
tu **te** laves etc.
il **se** lave
elle **se** lave
nous **nous** lavons
vous **vous** lavez
ils **se** lavent
elles **se** lavent

You must learn this kind of verb very carefully, especially the extra pronouns **me**, **te**, **se**, **se**, **nous**, **vous**, **se**, **se**.

More reflexive verbs

se brosser les cheveux to brush one's hair
se brosser les dents to brush one's teeth
se coucher to go to bed
se dépêcher to hurry
s'habiller to get dressed (this verb has **m'**, **t'**, **s'** in front of the '**h**')
se lever* to get up
se réveiller to wake up
se trouver to be (found)

* **There are some accent additions in the present tense of this verb:**
Je me lève, tu te lèves, il se lève, elle se lève, ils se lèvent, elles se lèvent (*but* **nous nous levons, vous vous levez – no accents**).

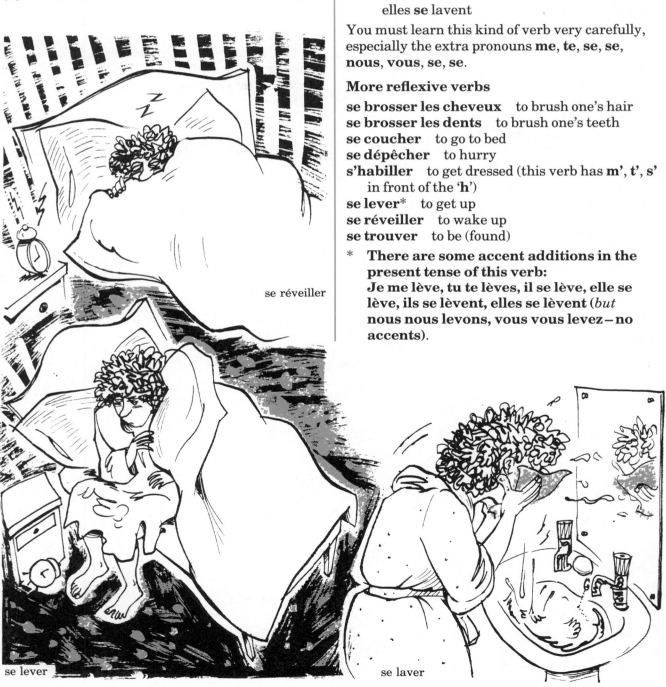

se réveiller

se lever

se laver

Le dimanche

Le dimanche je me réveille à neuf heures mais je ne me lève pas tout de suite. Je reste au lit jusqu'à neuf heures et demie. Alors je me lève puis je vais à la salle de bain qui se trouve à côté de ma chambre. Je me lave et je me brosse les dents. Puis je rentre dans ma chambre où je m'habille et me brosse les cheveux. Si je reste chez moi, je mets un blue-jean et un T-shirt. Mais si je dois rendre visite à mes grands-parents je mets une jolie robe car mes grands-parents n'aiment pas les blue-jeans. Si nous allons chez mes grands-parents en hiver ma mère dit toujours 'Mets ton manteau aujourd'hui. Il fait froid.' Mon père met son pardessus car il a toujours froid chez mes grands-parents.

'Dépêchez-vous,' dit mon père à ma mère et à moi. 'Vous êtes toujours en retard!'

New words

tout de suite   immediately
jusqu'à   until
à côté de   next to
rentrer   to go back
mettre   to put (on)
en retard   late

Unit 4 continued

New verb

mettre

N.B. single 't' in the singular

je mets   I put (on),
tu mets   etc.
il met
elle met
nous mettons
vous mettez
ils mettent
elles mettent

Command forms of reflexive verbs

In the passage earlier in this Unit Monsieur Gavarin said to Céline and her mother . . .

Dépêchez-vous   (Hurry up).

The command forms of reflexive verbs have the following additions . . .

dépêche-**toi**	hurry up (*used when speaking to one person in the familiar form*)
dépêchez-**vous**	hurry up (*plural and polite singular form*)
dépêchons-**nous**	let us hurry up

Telling the time

Do you remember how to tell the time in French? In the passage in this Unit Céline said . . .
Je me réveille **à neuf heures**.
and Je reste au lit jusqu'**à neuf heures et demie**.
Here are some of the main points to remember when expressing the time in French:

(a) for quarter past the hour add 'et quart'
e.g.   10.15   Il est dix heures **et quart**.

(b) for half past the hour add 'et demie'
e.g.   10.30   Il est dix heures **et demie**.

   except for 'midi' or 'minuit' when you use:
      12.30   Il est midi et **demi**.
      00.30   Il est minuit et **demi**.

(c) for quarter to the hour add 'moins le quart'
e.g.   01.45   Il est deux heures **moins le quart**.

(d) for minutes past the hour use numbers
e.g.   07.20   Il est sept heures **vingt**.

(e) for minutes to the hour use numbers with the word 'moins'
e.g.   07.40   Il est huit heures **moins vingt**.

If you need to revise Time more fully check back to Unit 15 in Volume 1.

Activités

1 Learn the verb **se laver** so that you can say and write it without looking at the book. Also learn its meanings in English.

2 The list on page 22 shows some more reflexive verbs that you will need to know. Learn them carefully.

3 Learn the new words and the verb 'mettre'.

4 Read the passage aloud in French then answer the questions in English.

(a) At what time does Céline normally wake up on Sundays?
(b) At what time does she get up?
(c) What does she do next?
(d) Where is the bathroom?
(e) What clothes does she put on if she is staying at home?
(f) What does she put on if she is going to visit her grandparents?
(g) Why?
(h) What does her mother tell her to do if it is cold?
(i) What does her father put on?
(j) What does her father always say to Céline and her mother?

5 Without looking at the verb 'mettre' above, complete the following sentences in French.

(a) Je .... mon manteau.
(b) Vous ...... votre manteau?
(c) Il ... son pardessus?
(d) Elle ... son manteau.
(e) Elles .... leurs chaussures.
(f) Tu .... ton chapeau?
(g) Ils .... leurs souliers.
(h) Nous .... nos gants.
(i) Je .... ma nouvelle robe.
(j) Il ... son gilet.

6 Do you remember the different articles of clothing you learnt in Volume 1? Now give the English meanings of the completed sentences in Activité 5.

7 Before attempting this Activité read again the section about reflexive verbs at the beginning of this Unit.

Now complete the sentences in the next column with the correct form of the verb. Say the answers aloud in French, then write the answers in your Record Book.

Activités continued

(a)
   (i) Elle (se réveiller) à huit heures.
   (ii) Nous (se laver) dans la salle de bain.
  (iii) Je (mettre) mon blue-jean.
  (iv) Ils (se lever) à sept heures.
   (v) Vous (se coucher) à dix heures.
  (vi) La salle de bain (se trouver) à côté de ma chambre.
 (vii) Elles (se dépêcher).
(viii) Tu (se coucher) à neuf heures et demie.
  (ix) Je (s'habiller) dans ma chambre.
   (x) Elle (se brosser) les cheveux.

(b) Now give the meaning of the completed sentences in English.

8 Answer the following questions about yourself in French. Remember to use 'Je me . . .' in the answer *if* the verb is reflexive.

(a) A quelle heure te réveilles-tu le dimanche?
(b) A quelle heure te réveilles-tu le lundi?
(c) Où t'habilles-tu?
(d) Où te laves-tu?
(e) Quels vêtements mets-tu le dimanche?
(f) Quels vêtements mets-tu le samedi?
(g) Mets-tu un manteau/pardessus quand il fait froid?
(h) Quels vêtements mets-tu quand il fait chaud?
(i) Te dépêches-tu pour aller à l'école?
(j) Te dépêches-tu pour rentrer de l'école?

9 Here are the command forms of some more reflexive verbs. Say what they mean in English.

(a) Lève-toi.
(b) Brosse-toi les dents.
(c) Couchez-vous.
(d) Levez-vous.
(e) Lavons-nous.

10 Now give the following commands in French.

(a) (*to a friend of your own age*) Wake up.
(b) (*to an adult*) Wake up.
(c) Let's get up.
(d) (*to a child*) Brush your hair.
(e) (*to several children*) Hurry up.

11 Here is a quick revision test to see how much you can remember!
Give in French the times shown opposite.
Use 'il est . . .' at the beginning of each one.

(f) 21.45   **(g)** 14.35   **(h)** 23.55
(i) 06.10   **(j)** 19.25

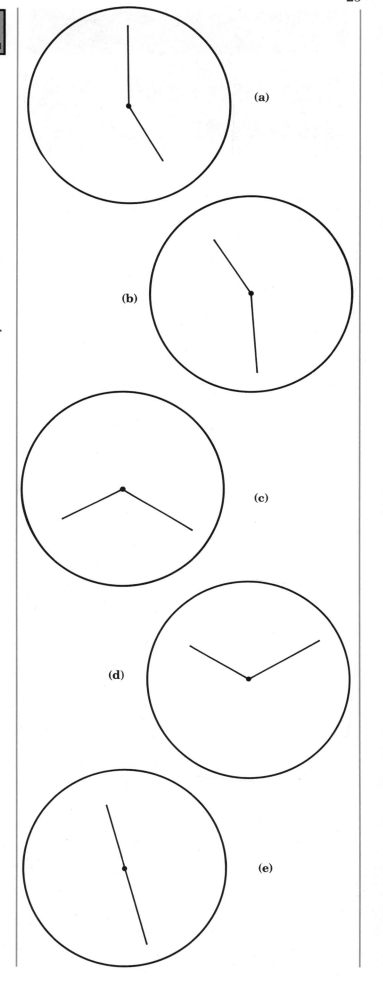

Unit 5

Les lettres/ Letters

In this unit you will learn:
(1) how to write simple personal letters in French;
(2) the verbs 'recevoir' (to receive) and 'écrire' (to write);
(3) more vocabulary about farms.

A letter to a friend

Here is a letter Céline received during the summer holidays from her friend Françoise.

New words
les nouvelles (f) news
aider to help
nourrir to feed
la sorte sort
une oie goose
le poulailler henhouse
jouer à cache-cache to play hide and seek
une étable cowshed
une écurie stable
la porcherie pigsty
faire des bêtises to play the fool
se mettre en colère to get angry
se baigner to bathe
une semaine week
s'intéresser à to be interested in

Vercors, le 3 août

Ma chère Céline,

Merci bien de ta gentille lettre. J'aime beaucoup recevoir de tes nouvelles. Moi aussi, je passe de très bonnes vacances chez mes grands-parents. Leur ferme se trouve à deux kilomètres de Vercors. Tous les matins j'aide mon grand-père à nourrir les animaux. Il y a toutes sortes d'animaux à la ferme – chevaux, vaches, moutons, cochons, oies, poules. J'aime surtout ramasser les œufs dans le poulailler.

Aujourd'hui mes petits cousins Vermorel vont arriver pour passer aussi quelques jours chez nos grands-parents. On s'amuse bien avec nos cousins. On joue à cache-cache dans l'étable, ou dans l'écurie et même dans la porcherie. Mais quelquefois Marc et Antoine font des bêtises et alors mon grand-père se met en colère. S'il fait très beau nous allons nous baigner dans la rivière. Marc a l'intention d'aller à la pêche tous les jours avec Antoine mais moi, je préfère rester avec les animaux.

Tu dis dans ta lettre que tu vas passer une semaine à Londres. Envoie-moi une carte postale des Palais du Parlement, s'il te plaît. Je m'intéresse beaucoup à l'architecture anglaise.

Écris-moi vite.

ton amie,
Françoise.

Écrire

At the end of Françoise's letter you saw . . .

> Ecris-moi vite.
>
> Write to me soon (quickly).

The verb 'écrire' (to write) has to be learnt carefully as it is different from other verbs that you have learnt.

Here is the present tense:

j'écris   I write,
tu écris   etc.
il écrit
elle écrit
nous écrivons
vous écrivez
ils écrivent
elles écrivent

Recevoir

Here is another useful verb for you

recevoir   to receive

Learn all the parts of the verb carefully as it does not follow the normal patterns which you learnt in Volume 1.

je reçois   I receive,
tu reçois   etc.
il reçoit
elle reçoit
nous recevons
vous recevez
ils reçoivent
elles reçoivent

N.B. the cedilla (¸) is required in all parts of the present tense except 'nous'/'vous'. The vowels 'e' and 'i' automatically 'soften' the letter 'c' (and 'g') and so the cedilla is not required in those forms. The cedilla reminds us to pronounce the letter 'c' as an 's'.

Writing to a French penfriend

One of the best ways of learning to write letters in French is to have a French correspondent. If you do not already have a French correspondent, ask your teacher at school if he/she is able to find one for you.

When you write to a French correspondent for the first time you should give him/her details about yourself, family, home and district. For example you should give . . .

your name	**je m'appelle . . .**
your age	**j'ai . . . ans**
how many brothers	**j'ai . . . frère(s)**
how many sisters	**j'ai . . . soeur(s)**
their ages	**mon frère . . . a . . . ans**
	ma soeur . . . a . . . ans

the name of your town/village **j'habite . . .** some information about the district

e.g. **C'est une ville industrielle**
   C'est un joli village à la campagne.
   C'est une station balnéaire*.
                                    etc.

*   **Une station balnéaire**   seaside resort/spa

Your French correspondent will almost certainly put his/her address on the back of the envelope and not at the top of the letter. Do not lose the envelope before you have made a note of his/her address.

Your letter should begin . . .

Cher . . .   (to a boy)   Dear . . .
Chère . . .   (to a girl)   Dear . . .

When you know your penfriend really well, perhaps when you have met personally, you may use . . .

Mon cher . . .
Ma chère . . .

as Françoise did in her letter to Céline.

Here is part of a letter from a French boy to his new English penfriend. He has written the first part of his letter in French.

Lyon, le 10 mars.

Cher Michael,

   Mon professeur d'anglais m'a donné ton nom et ton adresse. Je suis très content d'avoir un correspondant anglais. Je m'appelle Robert Duval. J'ai treize ans. J'ai un frère et une soeur. Mon frère Alain a douze ans et ma soeur Nadine a six ans. J'habite à Lyon. C'est une grande ville dans la vallée* du Rhône.

. . . .

Écris-moi vite
   Ton nouvel ami,
      Robert.

---

*   **la vallée**   valley
   la vallée du Rhône   the Rhône valley

When you write to your French penfriend you may also write at the end
   Écris-moi vite
followed by **Ton nouvel ami/Ta nouvelle amie** (*f*) the first time you write, but after that you should use one of the following after 'Écris-moi vite'.

   Amitiés
or **Amicalement**
or **Bien à toi.**
All three mean 'Best wishes'.

Activités

1 Learn the new words and then read the letter aloud in French.

2 Answer in English the following questions about the letter.

(a) What does Françoise say that she likes at the beginning of the letter?
(b) Where do her grand-parents live?
(c) What does Françoise help her grandfather to do?
(d) What does she especially like doing?
(e) What happens when Marc and Antoine play the fool?
(f) What do the children do if the weather is really fine?
(g) What do Marc and Antoine intend to do every day?
(h) What does Françoise prefer doing?
(i) How long is Céline going to stay in London?
(j) What does Françoise ask her to do at the end of the letter?

3 Learn the verb 'écrire' carefully and then complete the following sentences with the correct part of the verb.

(a) J' ..... beaucoup de lettres.
(b) Ils .... des cartes postales.
(c) Nous .... à nos amis.
(d) Elle ..... à son amie.
(e) Tu ..... beaucoup de lettres?
(f) Elles .... beaucoup de cartes postales.
(g) Vous .... à vos copains?
(h) Il ..... une lettre.
(i) Ils .... des lettres.
(j) Tu ..... à tes parents?

4 Now answer the following questions in French.

(a) As-tu un correspondant français?
(b) As-tu une correspondante française?
(c) Tu écris souvent des lettres?
(d) Tu écris souvent des cartes postales?
(e) Tu écris à tes grands-parents?

5 Complete the following sentences with the correct part of the verb 'recevoir'.

(a) Nous .... des lettres de nos amis.
(b) Je ...... une lettre de ma grand'mère.
(c) Elles .... des cartes postales de leurs amies.
(d) Tu ...... des cartes postales de tes amis?
(e) Ils .... des cartes postales.
(f) Elle ...... une lettre de sa copine.
(g) Vous .... des cartes postales?
(h) Il ...... des lettres de ses amis?
(i) Ils .... des lettres de leurs parents?
(j) Je ...... des cartes postales de mes amis.

6 Answer the following questions in French.

(a) Tu reçois des cartes postales de tes amis?
(b) Tu reçois des lettres de tes grands-parents?
(c) Tu reçois souvent des lettres?
(d) Ton frère reçoit souvent des lettres?
(e) Ta soeur reçoit souvent des cartes postales?

7 Write a letter to a French penfriend like the one given above. Begin as follows . . .

Cher (Chère) . . .
Mon professeur de français m'a donné . . .

Give details in French about yourself, family and town/village as shown in Robert's letter and end the letter with an appropriate ending in French.

Unit 6

Au bureau de poste/
At the post office

*I*n *this unit you will learn:*
(1) how to ask for directions to a post office;
(2) how to buy stamps in France;
(3) how to telephone in France;
(4) the verb 'acheter' (to buy).

Unit 6 continued

New words

avant de   before
en bas   down below/on the bottom
la boîte aux lettres   letter-box
le facteur   postman
la fente   slot
fermé   closed
le guichet   counter/window
la dernière levée   the last collection
les heures des levées   the times of collection
les imprimés   printed matter
mettre à la poste }
poster } to post
ouvert   open
par exemple   for example
P et T (Postes et Télécommunications)   Post Office
seulement   only
le bureau de tabac   tobacconist's
tarif réduit   reduced rate/cheap rate
le timbre-poste   postage stamp (*plural* les timbres-poste)

Pour mettre une lettre à la poste

Avant de mettre une lettre ou une carte postale à la poste, on doit d'abord acheter un timbre-poste.

On peut acheter les timbres-poste dans un bureau de tabac ou au bureau de poste. Si vous ne trouvez pas de bureau de poste, demandez à un passant . . .
'Pardon monsieur (madame), pour aller au bureau de poste, s'il vous plaît?'

Si vous cherchez un bureau de tabac, demandez à un passant . . .
'Pardon monsieur (madame), pour aller au bureau de tabac s'il vous plaît?'

Si vous cherchez une boîte aux lettres, demandez à un passant . . .
'Pardon monsieur (madame), y a-t-il une boîte aux lettres près d'ici?'

En France les boîtes aux lettres sont jaunes. Regardez cette photo. Il y a toujours une boîte aux lettres au bureau de poste mais regardez bien la boîte. Il y a presque toujours deux fentes. Par exemple . . .

TARIF RÉDUIT	TARIF NORMAL

ou

PARIS SEULEMENT	AUTRES DESTINATIONS

ou

LETTRES	IMPRIMÉS

et en bas. . .
NE JETER DANS CETTE BOÎTE
NI GROSSES LETTRES NI IMPRIMÉS

Pour acheter un timbre-poste dans le bureau de tabac ou au bureau de poste, dites à l'employé . . .
'C'est combien pour envoyer une lettre/une carte postale en Grande-Bretagne, s'il vous plaît monsieur (madame)?'

Si vous allez dans un grand bureau de poste, on va peut-etre dire . . .
'Pour les timbres, c'est au guichet 5.'

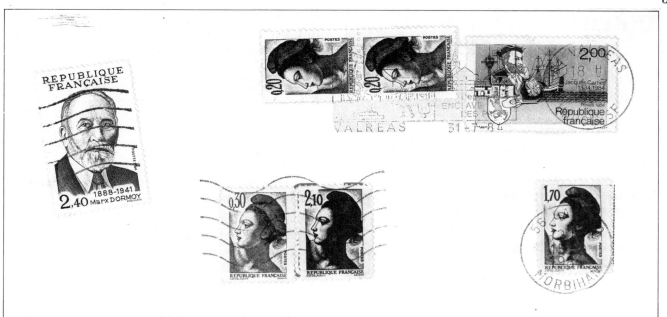

Voici des timbres-poste

Céline achète des timbres-poste en ville. Elle va envoyer une lettre à sa copine Françoise. Les deux jeunes filles s'écrivent souvent pendant les grandes vacances. Elles envoient aussi des cartes postales à toutes leurs amies. Mais Marc n'écrit pas de lettres. Il envoie rarement une carte postale à son copain Frédéric. Il préfère le téléphone. Marc reçoit de temps en temps une lettre de ses grands-parents et le jour de son anniversaire il reçoit toujours un joli cadeau. Sur le paquet il y a toujours un timbre-poste intéressant. Marc aime bien collectionner les timbres-poste. Il a une belle collection.

New words

s'écrire to write to each other
pendant during
rarement rarely
le téléphone telephone
le cadeau present
intéressant interesting
collectionner to collect
la collection collection

Acheter

Here is the new verb 'acheter' (to buy). Learn all the parts carefully, remembering especially those parts which have accents.

j'achète I buy
tu achètes you (*singular*) buy
il achète he buys
elle achète she buys
nous achetons we buy
vous achetez you (*plural and polite singular*) buy
ils achètent they (*masc.*) buy
elles achètent they (*fem.*) buy

Unit 6 continued

Pour téléphoner en France

Voici deux cabines téléphoniques.

En France on peut téléphoner au bureau de poste, dans une cabine téléphonique ou dans un café.
Si vous allez téléphoner dans un café, demandez un jeton au garçon.
Dans une cabine téléphonique il y a deux fentes pour les pièces de monnaie – 5F (cinq francs)
1F (un franc)
(N.B. the ½F and 20c are no longer used.)

New words

une cabine téléphonique   telephone kiosk
téléphoner   to telephone
un jeton   a disc
une pièce de monnaie   coin

Here are some more useful words about telephoning in France:

l'annuaire du téléphone
le 'Bottin' } telephone directory
le cadran   dial
le récepteur   the receiver (*also* **le combiné**)
la tonalité   the dialling tone

and here are some instructions you might see inside the telephone kiosk:
(1) **Introduisez dans la fente 1F.**
   (Insert 1F in the slot)
(2) **Décrochez le combiné.**
   (Lift the receiver)
(3) **Attendez la tonalité.**
   (Wait for the dialling tone)
(4) **Composez le numéro.**
   (Dial the number)
(5) **Appuyez sur le bouton A.**
   (Press button A)

If you wish to telephone to Great Britain from France, you may use a telephone kiosk which takes 5F coins. If you are unsure about using a phone box, go to the local post office to make the call. They will dial the number for you and you will pay after making the call.

Activités

1 Learn all the new words before reading the passage 'Posting a letter in France'.

2 Answer the following questions in English.

(a) Where can stamps be bought in France?
(b) What colour are postboxes in France?
(c) If you wanted to post a letter to Great Britain, which slot would you use 'PARIS SEULEMENT' or 'AUTRES DESTINATIONS'?
(d) If you wanted to send a postcard to your family, which slot would you use 'LETTRES' or 'IMPRIMÉS'?
(e) What may you not post where there is the following:

NE JETER DANS CETTE BOÎTE
NI GROSSES LETTRES NI IMPRIMÉS?

(**ni . . . ni . . .** means 'neither . . . nor . . .').

3 Learn all the new words, then answer the following questions in English.

(a) Where is Céline?
(b) What is she doing?
(c) What is she going to do?
(d) What do Céline and Françoise often do during the summer holidays?
(e) Who do they send postcards to?
(f) Who does Marc write letters to?
(g) Who does he send postcards to?
(h) How often?
(i) What is always on the parcel Marc receives from his grandparents?
(j) What does Marc like doing?

4 Complete the following sentences with the correct part of the verb 'acheter'.

(a) Ils .... des timbres-poste.
(b) Nous ....des cartes postales.
(c) Tu .... un timbre-poste?
(d) J' ...... trois timbres-poste.
(e) Elles .... de jolis cadeaux*.
(f) Il ...... des timbres-poste.

(g) Vous .... des timbres-poste en ville?
(h) Elle ...... des timbres-poste au bureau de tabac.
(i) Tu .... des cartes postales au bureau de tabac?
(j) J' ...... des timbres-poste au bureau de tabac.

* **'cadeaux' is the plural of 'cadeau'.**

5 Answer the following questions in French.

(a) Tu achètes des cartes postales?
(b) Tu achètes des timbres-poste?
(c) Tu achètes des timbres-poste au bureau de tabac?
(d) Ton père achète des timbres-poste?
(e) Ton père envoie des cartes postales?
(f) Ta mère achète des timbres-poste au bureau de tabac?
(g) Tu préfères le téléphone?
(h) Tu collectionnes les timbres-poste?
(i) Tu reçois souvent des cadeaux?
(j) A qui écris-tu des lettres?

6 What would you say in French to ask for the following information?

(a) Is there a post office near here, please?
(b) How do I get to the post office, please?
(c) How much is it to send a postcard to Great Britain, please?
(d) How much is it to send a letter to Great Britain, please?
(e) Is there a postbox near here, please?
(f) When is the last collection?

In answer to the questions above, you might hear the following answers. Say in English what information you are being given.

(g) Oui, là-bas, à droite.
(h) Prenez la deuxième rue à gauche.
(i) Un franc soixante-dix.
(j) Deux francs quarante.
(k) Oui, là-bas, en face de la banque.
(l) A dix-huit heures trente.

7 Learn all the new words and especially the meaning of the instructions inside a telephone kiosk.

Unit 7

Les avis et les instructions/ Notices and instructions

In this unit you will:
(1) revise and learn more about the command form of verbs;
(2) revise and learn more about numbers in French;
(3) learn the present tense of the verb 'prendre' (to take);
(4) practise giving and understanding certain commands in French.

Le premier avril

Aujourd'hui c'est le premier avril. Céline et Marc vont au collège. C'est un jour que les enfants aiment bien car ils vont jouer un tour à leurs amis. 'Mettons un poisson d'avril dans le dos du censeur avant les classes,' dit Marc.

Au collège Marc est en sixième et Céline est en seconde. Il y a deux mille élèves au collège. Tous les matins Céline et Marc doivent traverser la ville pour arriver au collège. Quand ils arrivent au passage clouté, ils s'arrêtent. Puis quand les feux sont au vert, ils traversent sur le passage clouté. On voit les mots PASSEZ PIÉTONS sur le feu vert. 'Dépêche-toi, nous sommes en retard,' dit Céline à son frère.

Marc et Céline habitent à un kilomètre du collège et ils sont souvent parmi les derniers à arriver. Devant leur maison il y a une affiche DÉFENSE DE STATIONNER. Mais on ne fait pas attention car il y a toujours des voitures qui stationnent devant leur maison!

Ce matin ils se dépêchent pour arriver à l'heure. Quelquefois ils prennent l'autobus pour aller au collège mais aujourd'hui il y a une grève d'autobus. Voilà pourquoi ils vont au collège à pied. Tout à coup Céline voit les mains sales de Marc. 'N'oublie pas de te laver les mains avant les classes et peigne-toi les cheveux. Ne mets pas de poisson d'avril dans le dos du censeur.'

'OK Boss!' dit Marc.

'Parle français, pas américain!' répond Céline.

New words

jouer un tour à   to play a trick on
un poisson d'avril   an April fool trick (children try to stick a paper fish on the back of their friends without their noticing)
le dos   the back
le censeur   Deputy Head
sixième   sixth ⎫
seconde   second ⎭ (N.B. French secondary schools number their forms in inverse order. Therefore, 'sixième' is the equivalent of the first form in Great Britain)

mille   thousand

le passage clouté   pedestrian crossing
s'arrêter   to stop
les feux   traffic-lights
le mot   word
le piéton   pedestrian
parmi   amongst
une affiche   notice
Défense de . . .   No . . .
stationner   to park
faire attention   to pay attention
à l'heure   on time
la grève   strike
pourquoi   why
à pied   on foot
la main   hand
sale   dirty
se peigner les cheveux   to comb one's hair

Numbers

Do you remember the numbers you learnt in Volume 1?

Here are some more numbers.

(a) 200 **deux cents**
   300 **trois cents**   etc.

An 's' is added to 'cent' when there is *no* other number following

But . . .
201 deux **cent** un
245 deux **cent** quarante-cinq   etc.

The 's' is omitted on the word 'cent' when another number follows.

(b) 1000 **mille**
   2000 **deux mille**
   3000 **trois mille**
   N.B. There is no 's' here on the word 'mille'. (When an 's' is added to 'mille' it means 'miles'.)

(c) 1 000 000 **un million**
   2 000 000 **deux millions**   etc.

'Premier' and 'dernier'

In the passage at the beginning of this unit, you saw the word 'dernier' (last). The opposite of this word is 'premier' (first).

Both words have a special feminine form:

première   **dernière**

You also saw the word **second(e)**. Another word which means 'second' is **deuxième**.

Here are some more ordinal numbers (first, second, third, etc.):

troisième   third
quatrième   fourth
cinquième   fifth, etc.

These words are used to show 'order' or 'position' but are *not* used for dates except 'premier' e.g., 'le premier mai' (but, 'le deux mai', 'le trois mai', etc.).

Unit 7 *continued*

The verb 'prendre' (to take)

You have already learnt part of this verb in Volume 1:

> Pre*n*ez la première rue à gauche
> (Take the first street on the left).

And in the passage at the beginning of this Unit you saw . . .

> Ils **prennent** l'autobus
> (They take the bus).

The verb 'prendre' is irregular and you must learn all the parts carefully.

je prends   I take,
tu prends   etc.
il prend
elle prend
nous prenons
vous prenez
ils pre**nn**ent
elles pre**nn**ent

Command forms of 'prendre'

The command forms of the verb 'prendre' are:

Prends   to one person (of your own age or whom you know well)
Prenez   to more than one, person or polite singular form
Prenons   let us take

Commands and instructions

Here are some more commands/instructions which you might see in France. Learn them carefully and then tell your parents what they mean.

Allumez vos phares   (Switch on your headlights)
Eteignez vos phares   (Switch off your headlights)
R.S.V.P/Répondez s'il vous plaît   (Please reply)
Ne traversez pas   (Don't cross)
N'oubliez pas de composter   (Don't forget to use the automatic ticket-punching machine)

and if you see the following signs . . .

> DÉFENSE DE . . .
> or INTERDIT DE . . .

it means that YOU MUST NOT . . .

e.g.   **Défense d'entrer**   No entry

Activités

1 Learn all the new words.

2 Read the passage aloud in French, then answer the following questions by choosing which answer you think is the most appropriate.

(a) Where are Marc and Céline going?
   (i) to college
   (ii) to school
   (iii) shopping
   (iv) home

(b) Why do they like this particular day?
   (i) They are going on holiday.
   (ii) They are going on a tour.
   (iii) They are going to play with their friends.
   (iv) They are going to play tricks on their friends.

(c) When is Marc hoping to see the Deputy Head?
   (i) before school
   (ii) after school
   (iii) during lessons
   (iv) at break time

(d) What form is Céline in? (Give the British equivalent.)
   (i) First
   (ii) Second
   (iii) Fifth
   (iv) Sixth

(e) How many pupils are there in their school?
   (i) two hundred
   (ii) two thousand
   (iii) six hundred
   (iv) six thousand

(f) Why do they stop on their way to school?
   (i) The traffic lights are at red.
   (ii) There is a strike.
   (iii) They are waiting for the bus.
   (iv) They are waiting for their friends.

(g) Marc and Céline often arrive at school . . .
   (i) the first
   (ii) the last
   (iii) with their friends
   (iv) after the bell

(h) What does the sign say in front of their house?
   (i) To the station
   (ii) Ministry of Defence
   (iii) Bus stop
   (iv) No parking

(i) What does Céline suddenly notice before arriving at school?
   (i) Marc's dirty hands
   (ii) Marc's dirty shoes
   (iii) A sale in a clothes shop
   (iv) She has forgotten her books

(j) What does she say to Marc?
   (i) Wait a minute.
   (ii) Run back home for me.
   (iii) Wash your face.
   (iv) Comb your hair.

3 What is the French for . . .

   8   16   21   39   54   77   84   93   99   100

4 Say the following numbers aloud in French, then write them in words in French . . .

   500   436   728   4,000   3,000,000

5 Give the French for . . .

(a) the first day
(b) the last bus
(c) the fourth street
(d) the third house
(e) the fifth of June

6 Complete the following sentences with the correct part of 'prendre'.

(a) Nous .... l'autobus.
(b) Ils .... l'autobus.
(c) Elle ..... la première rue à droite.
(d) Tu ...... la deuxième rue à droite.
(e) Elles .... la troisième rue à gauche.
(f) Je ...... le train.
(g) Vous ...... le train.
(h) Il ..... ses livres.
(i) Je ...... un café.
(j) Elles .... des glaces.

7 Before attempting this Activité check again Unit 21 in Volume 1 and Unit 4 in this Volume.

Give the following commands in French.

(a) (*to a friend*) Take the first street on the right.
(b) Let us take the bus.
(c) (*to a group of people*) Take the second street on the left.
(d) (*to a friend*) Wake up.
(e) Let us go to town.

Unit 8

Au restaurant/ At the restaurant

In this unit you will learn:
(1) the verbs 'pouvoir' (to be able), 'vouloir' (to wish/want), 'savoir' (to know);
(2) how to read a menu in French;
(3) how to order a meal in French;
(4) how to tell someone which dishes you like/dislike.

Un menu

Voici un menu français.

MENU À 65F

CRUDITÉS
OEUFS À LA MAYONNAISE
RADIS AU BEURRE
SALADES DE TOMATES

•

CÔTELETTE DE PORC
POULET RÔTI
OMELETTE AU JAMBON

•

POMMES FRITES
HARICOTS VERTS

•

SALADE

•

FROMAGE

•

GLACES
TARTE AUX FRAISES
FRUITS

Can you read the menu? Would you know what to choose?

Here is the menu in English.

Chopped raw vegetables
(*e.g., tomatoes, peppers, carrots, etc.*)
Hard boiled eggs with mayonnaise
Radishes and butter
Tomato salad

•

Pork chop
Roast chicken
Ham omelette

French fried potatoes
Beans (green)

•

Green salad

•

Cheese

•

Ices
Strawberry tart
Fruit

L'anniversaire de Céline

Savez-vous quel jour nous sommes aujourd'hui? C'est le dix mars, l'anniversaire de Céline. La famille Gavarin va fêter son anniversaire au restaurant. Les enfants aiment beaucoup manger dans un restaurant. Quand la famille Gavarin entre dans le restaurant, Monsieur Gavarin dit au garçon, 'Une table pour quatre personnes, s'il vous plaît.'

Le garçon répond, 'Bien, monsieur. Voilà une table libre près de la fenêtre.'

La famille se met à table.

'Voulez-vous voir le menu, monsieur?' demande le garçon.

Monsieur Gavarin prend le menu et demande à sa femme, 'Qu'est-ce que tu veux prendre, chérie?'

'Alors, je prends les crudités, et après, une omelette au jambon et des haricots verts. Je sais que les omelettes sont bonnes ici,' répond Madame Gavarin.

Puis Monsieur Gavarin se tourne vers les enfants, 'Et les enfants?'

'Moi, je voudrais une salade de tomates, puis du poulet rôti avec des frites, s'il te plaît, papa,' dit Céline.

'Et toi, Marc, tu as faim? Qu'est-ce que tu vas prendre?' demande Monsieur Gavarin.

'J'ai grand' faim, papa. Je voudrais une salade de tomates aussi, puis une côtelette de porc et des haricots verts, s'il te plaît,' dit Marc.

'J'ai chaud dans cette salle,' dit Madame Gavarin. 'Pouvons-nous nous mettre à la terrasse, chéri?'

'Bien sûr,' dit Monsieur Gavarin.

Il appelle le garçon. 'Nous voulons manger à la terrasse,' dit Monsieur Gavarin.

'Bien, monsieur, il y a une table libre à la terrasse, à gauche,' répond le garçon.

New words

 fêter   to celebrate
 *savoir   to know
 *vouloir   to wish/want
 se tourner   to turn towards
 *pouvoir   to be able
 se mettre   to sit (lit. to place oneself)

*   **You will learn the different parts of these verbs in this Unit.**

'Pouvoir' and 'vouloir'

In the passage opposite you saw three new verbs: 'pouvoir', 'vouloir' and 'savoir'. Here is the present tense of the verbs 'pouvoir' and 'vouloir'.

pouvoir   to be able

je peux	I can, am able,
tu peux	etc.
il peut	
elle peut	
nous pouvons	
vous pouvez	
ils peuvent	
elles peuvent	

vouloir   to wish/want

je veux	I wish/want,
tu veux	etc.
il veut	
elle veut	
nous voulons	
vous voulez	
ils veulent	
elles veulent	

Extra note: 'pouvoir'

You may sometimes hear the following in conversation:

Puis-je . . .?   (Can I . . .?)
e.g.   **Puis-je** vous aider? (Can I help you?)

It is part of the verb 'pouvoir' but almost always confined to the question form.

'Savoir'

The third new verb in the passage was 'savoir' (to know). Here are the different parts of the present tense.

savoir	to know (how to)
je sais	I know,
tu sais	etc.
il sait	
elle sait	
nous savons	
vous savez	
ils savent	
elles savent	

More menu choices

Here are some more items you might see on menus every day in France.

(les)	**hors-d'oeuvres variés**	
	mixed meat, fish and vegetable starter	
(la)	**charcuterie** mixed cold meat starter	
(le)	**paté maison** home-made paté	
(le)	**melon** melon	
(le)	**potage** soup	

•

(le)	**gigot d'agneau** leg of lamb	
(le)	**canard à l'orange**	
	duck with orange sauce	
(le)	**jambon** ham	
(les)	**rognons** kidneys	
(le)	**steak grillé** grilled steak	
(une)	**escalope de veau** veal escalope	

•

(les)	**artichauts** artichokes	
(les)	**asperges** asparagus	
(les)	**carottes** carrots	
(les)	**choux de Bruxelles** Brussels sprouts	
(le)	**chou-fleur** cauliflower	
(les)	**épinards** spinach	
(les)	**petits pois** peas	
(les)	**pommes à l'anglaise** boiled potatoes	

•

(l')	**ananas** pineapple	
(la)	**crème-caramel** cream caramel dessert	
(les)	**crêpes** pancakes	
(les)	**pâtisseries** pastries	

Activités

1 Learn all the new words then choose ('prendre') from the French menu the dishes you would most like to order. Say aloud in French . . .

je prends . . . (give your choice in French).

2 Read the passage aloud in French, then answer the following questions in English.

(a) What is the date in the passage above?
(b) Why is it a special day?
(c) Where are the family?
(d) What does Madame Gavarin order for her main course?
(e) What does Céline order for her main course?
(f) What vegetables does Marc want?
(g) Where does the family sit at first?
(h) Why does Madame Gavarin want to move?
(i) Where does she want to sit?
(j) Where does the waiter tell them to sit?

3 Learn all the parts of the present tense of 'pouvoir' and 'vouloir', then complete the sentences below with the correct part of the verb.

(a) Nous v...... manger au restaurant.
(b) Ils v...... manger à la terrasse.
(c) Je v... fêter mon anniversaire au restaurant.
(d) Tu p... venir*?
(e) Vous v..... venir?
(f) Elles p...... aller au cinéma.
(g) Tu v... de la salade?
(h) Il p... fêter son anniversaire au restaurant.
(i) Elle v... se mettre à la terrasse.
(j) On p... manger au restaurant.

* **venir** to come

4 Learn all the parts of 'savoir' carefully and then complete the sentences below with the correct part of the verb.

(a) Je s... préparer une omelette.
(b) Vous s.... préparer une omelette?
(c) Elle s... préparer une omelette au jambon.
(d) Tu s... faire la cuisine*?
(e) Ils s..... préparer une salade de tomates.

* **faire la cuisine** to cook

5 Now say what the completed sentences in Activités 3 and 4 mean in English.

6 Choose one item from each of the sections in 'More menu choices' and say . . .

(a) what you like. Begin with 'j'aime . . .'
e.g. **J'aime le melon.**
(b) what you don't like. Begin with 'je n'aime pas . . .'
e.g. **Je n'aime pas le potage.**

7 You are in a restaurant in France with your family.

(a) Ask the waiter for a table for five people, please.
(b) Ask him if you can sit outside.
(c) Say you would like to see the menu.
(d) Ask your parents (in French) what they would like to have.
(e) Ask your mother (in French) if she is cold.
(f) Tell the waiter that you would like soup, steak and French fried potatoes, and an ice-cream, please.
(g) Ask for the bill.
(h) Ask if the service charge is included.

You will find some useful phrases in the passage in this unit and also Unit 20 in Volume 1.

Unit 9

En famille/ en visite
At home/visiting

In this unit you will:
(1) learn more about family relationships;
(2) learn more about introductions and greetings;
(3) learn the verb 'connaître' (to know/to be acquainted with);
(4) practise making requests and expressing regret.

Voici l'arbre généalogique de la famille Gavarin et de la famille Latille

Here are the Gavarin and Latille family trees.

Monsieur et Madame Pierre Gavarin sont les grands-parents de Céline et de Marc.

Monsieur et Madame Paul Baudoin ont cinq petits-enfants – Céline, Marc, Antoine, Marie-Jeanne, Sylviane.

Monsieur Philippe Gavarin a un neveu et deux nièces.

Suzanne Latille est la tante de Céline et de Marc.

Michel Latille est l'oncle de Céline et de Marc.

New words

les petits-enfants grandchildren
un neveu nephew (*pl.* neveux)
une nièce niece
la tante aunt
l'oncle uncle

Pierre Gavarin — Janine   Paul Baudoin — Agnès

Philippe Gavarin — Paulette   Suzanne — Michel Latille

Céline   Marc   Antoine   Marie-Jeanne   Sylviane

Unit 9 continued

Introducing people

In Volume 1 you learnt how to introduce people by using 'voici'.

e.g. **Voici ma mère** (Here is my mother)

You may also say (and you are sure to hear)

Je te présente . . . (*when speaking to someone of your own age*)

or **Je vous présente . . .** (*when speaking to an adult who is not a relative or to more than one person*)

e.g. **Je vous présente mon père.**

'Connaître'

Before introducing people you might wish to ask if they already know each other. The verb 'connaître' is used when speaking about people.

Here are the different parts of the verb.

connaître to know

je connais I know,
tu connais etc.
il connaît
elle connaît
nous connaissons
vous connaissez
ils connaissent
elles connaissent

Responding to an introduction

After you have been introduced to someone in French, you will find that there are several ways of responding 'Pleased to meet you'. Look at the examples on these pages.

Antoine (speaking to Marc): Je te présente Paul.
Paul (speaking to Marc): **Bonjour**, Marc.
Marc (speaking to Paul): **Bonjour**, Paul.

Marc: Papa, je te présente Paul.
Paul: **Enchanté**, monsieur.

Marc: Maman, je te présente Paul.
Paul: **Heureux de faire votre connaissance**, Madame.

(a) When being introduced to someone of your own age, use . . . **Bonjour** (and include the person's name).

(b) When being introduced to an adult use . . .

Enchanté, Monsieur/Madame (if you are a boy).

Enchantée, Monsieur/Madame (if you are a girl).

or **Heureux de faire votre connaissance, Monsieur/Madame** (if you are a boy).

Heureuse de faire votre connaissance Monsieur/Madame (if you are a girl).

Requests

You already know how to make simple requests in French. Here are some of the phrases you might use:

S'il te plaît/s'il vous plaît

e.g. Un kilo de pommes, **s'il vous plaît**.
(when shopping in the market)

Je voudrais . . .

e.g. **Je voudrais** une chambre à deux lits.
(when booking a hotel room)

Vous voulez . . .

e.g. **Vous voulez** me passer du pain?
(when asking for bread during a meal)

Tu peux/vous pouvez . . .

e.g. Tu **peux** me passer le journal?
(when asking someone to pass you the newspaper)

Donnez-moi . . .

e.g. **Donnez-moi** un coca-cola, s'il vous plaît.
(when ordering a drink in a café)

Expressing regret

If you need to apologize for something in French you may use . . .

Pardon

or **Excuse-moi** (*to a friend*)

or **Excusez-moi** (*to an adult or to a group of people*)

or **Je m'excuse**

or **Je suis désolé(e)** (Very sorry)

or **Je regrette . . .**

e.g. Je regrette d'être en retard.
(apologizing for being late)

In answer to your apology you might hear the following . . .

Je t'en prie ⎫	⎧ Please do!
Je vous en prie ⎭	⎩ My pleasure
or **Ce n'est pas grave**	It isn't serious.
or **Ça ne fait rien**	It doesn't matter.
or **Il n'y a pas de mal**	No harm done!

They are all telling you that '*it doesn't matter*'.

Activités

1 In your Record Book draw your own family tree. Include your four grandparents, your parents and their brothers and sisters, and your first cousins. Write one sentence in French about each member of the family tree.

2 Answer the following questions in French.

(a) Combien de frères as-tu?
(b) Combien de soeurs as-tu?
(c) As-tu des neveux?
(d) As-tu des nièces?
(e) Combien de cousins as-tu?
(f) Combien de cousines as-tu?

3 How would you introduce the following people in French.

(a) Your mother (*to a friend of your own age*)
(b) Your mother (*to several friends*)
(c) Your brother (*to an adult who is not a relative*)
(d) Your brother (*to a friend of your own age*)
(e) Your sister (*to a friend of your own age*)
(f) Your aunt (*to an adult who is not a relative*)
(g) Your uncle (*to a group of friends*)
(h) Your grandmother (*to a friend of your own age*)
(i) Your grandfather (*to a friend of your own age*)
(j) Your cousin (female) (*to a group of friends*)

4 Learn all the parts of the verb 'connaître' carefully and remember the accent (circumflex) in the infinitive and il/elle form.

5 Complete the sentences below with the correct part of 'connaître'.

(a) Ils .... mon père.
(b) Je .... son père.
(c) Vous .... ma mère?
(d) Elle .... ma soeur.
(e) Tu .... mes grands-parents?
(f) Elles .... ma tante.
(g) Il .... mon oncle.
(h) Nous .... vos cousins.
(i) Elle .... votre nièce.
(j) Ils .... ton grande-père.

6 The forms **Tu connais . . .?**
and **Vous connaissez . . .?**
are frequently used when asking if you know someone. Use them in the following questions.

Ask someone in French if he/she knows . . .
e.g. Your aunt (*asking a friend*) **Tu connais ma tante?**

(a) Your father (*asking a friend of your own age*)
(b) Your mother (*asking an adult*)
(c) Your brother (*asking a friend*)
(d) Your sister (*asking a friend*)
(e) Your uncle (*asking an adult*)

7 What would you say in French if you were introduced to the following people?
Use 'monsieur' or 'madame' except in (a) and (b).

(a) Marc
(b) Céline
(c) Monsieur Gavarin
(d) Madame Gavarin
(e) your penfriend's French teacher (male)
(f) your penfriend's French teacher (female)
(g) your penfriend's grandmother
(h) your penfriend's grandfather
(i) your penfriend's uncle
(j) your penfriend's aunt

8 Make the following requests in French.

(a) Give me a chocolate ice-cream, please.
(b) I would like steak and chips, please.
(c) A litre of milk, please.
(d) Will you pass me the salt (le sel), please.
(e) Can you pass me the bread, please.

9 What would you say in French in the following situations.
e.g. You have stepped on a lady's foot.
Oh, pardon, madame.

(a) You have stepped on a man's foot.

(b) Someone has stepped on your foot, he/she apologizes and you tell him/her that it does not matter.

(c) You apologize for being late.
(d) Someone apologizes to you for being late and you tell him/her that it doesn't matter.
(e) You have broken something. You apologize to your friend's mother.

Unit 10

La santé/Health et les maladies/Illness

In this unit you will learn:
(1) how to tell someone that you are unwell;
(2) how to get help if you are feeling unwell;
(3) various parts of the body in French;
(4) the expression 'il faut' (it is necessary).

le bras the arm
la cheville ankle
le dos back
la poitrine chest
le coude elbow
le doigt finger
le pied foot
la main hand
la tête head
le genou knee
la jambe leg
le cou neck
une épaule shoulder
l'estomac ⎱ stomach
le ventre ⎰
la gorge throat
le pouce thumb
l'orteil (*m*) toe
le poignet wrist

la joue cheek
le menton chin
une oreille ear
un oeil eye
les yeux eyes
la figure ⎱ face
le visage ⎰
le front forehead
les cheveux (*mpl*) hair
la lèvre lip
la bouche mouth
le nez nose
la langue tongue
la dent tooth

Unit 10 continued

Telling someone you are unwell

If you are feeling unwell, you should say . . .

Je suis souffrant(e).

If you are ill, you should say . . .

Je suis malade.

If you think you (or anyone else) should see a doctor, you should say . . .

Il faut consulter un médecin.

'Il faut' is a very useful expression to use. It is followed by an infinitive and can be used to refer to different people.

If you want to ask someone how he/she is, you could say . . .

    Ça va?
or **Comment vas-tu?** (*to a friend*)
or **Comment allez-vous?** (*to an adult who is not a relative*)

If you want to ask them if they are unwell, you could say . . .

    Tu es souffrant(e)? (*to a friend*)
or **Vous êtes souffrant(e)?** (*to an adult who is not a relative*)

If you want to ask them if they are ill, you could say . . .

    Tu es malade? (*to a friend*)
or **Vous êtes malade?** (*to an adult who is not a relative*)
or **Tu as mal?** ⎫
or **Vous avez mal?** ⎬ Are you in pain?

If you want to tell someone which part of your body hurts, you should say . . .

    J'ai mal à . . .
e.g. J'ai mal à la tête. (I have a headache.)
      J'ai mal à la gorge. (My throat is sore.)
      J'ai mal au pied. (My foot hurts.)

Here are two more expressions to learn . . .
J'ai de la fièvre (I have a high temperature)
J'ai mal au coeur (I feel sick).

At the doctor's

If you are ill on holiday in France, you may need to see a doctor. You will have to pay the doctor a consultation fee. Before going to France you should take out an insurance policy. You may also be eligible to obtain from the DHSS (Department of Health and Social Security) a form which will enable you to claim up to 70 per cent of the cost incurred of any medical fees.

The doctor in France will probably ask you one or more of the following questions . . .

(1) **Qu'est-ce qui ne va pas?**
    What is the matter?

(2) **Où as-tu mal?**
    Where do you hurt?

(3) **Ouvrez la bouche.**
    Open your mouth.

The doctor might then tell you . . .

Vous êtes enrhumé. (You have a cold.)
Vous avez la grippe. (You have 'flu.)
Il faut rester au lit deux ou trois jours.
(You must stay in bed for two or three days.)
Je vais vous donner une ordonnance.
(I will give you a prescription.)

A la pharmacie

For minor ailments in France, you may consult the local chemist. He is trained to give advice on health matters which do not require the attention of a doctor. You do not pay him a consultation fee, but he will probably suggest some medication from his shop for which you will have to pay.

Here are some of the minor ailments which you might have on holiday:

une blessure a cut
un bleu a bruise
les brûlures d'estomac indigestion
des coups de soleil sunburn
une crise de foie an upset stomach/sickness/diarrhoea

Read the following conversation aloud in French with a friend or one of your parents.

Touriste: Bonjour, monsieur. J'ai un coup de soleil. J'ai mal à la tête et au dos. Pouvez-vous me prescrire quelque chose?

Pharmacien: Oui, il fait très, très chaud ici. Vous n'êtes pas accoutumée au soleil? Voici une crème. Vous devez l'appliquer trois fois par jour.

Touriste: Merci, monsieur. Ça coûte combien?

New words

prescrire to prescribe
quelque chose something
accoutumé accustomed to
une crème a cream
appliquer to apply
la fois time
par jour each day

Activités

1 Learn all the new words.

2 Cut out two large human figures from a magazine. (Ask permission first!)
Stick them on to cardboard.
Now cut out lots of cardboard rectangles and write the French words for the various parts of the body on them. Make two cards for each part of the body.
You can now play the following speed game with a friend or with one of your parents. Each player has one of the figures and a pile of name-cards. At the word 'Go' you each race to label the parts of the body with their correct name-cards. The first one to finish correctly is the winner. If you wish to have more people playing at the same time, make more figures and more name-cards. Do make sure at the end of the game that the figure has been labelled correctly.

3 Learn carefully all of the expressions about feeling unwell.

4 What would you say in French to convey the following information?

(a) I feel unwell.
(b) Are you ill? (*to a friend*)
(c) You should consult a doctor.
(d) How are you? (*to a friend*)
(e) I am ill.
(f) I have a headache.
(g) My back hurts.
(h) I have earache.
(i) Are you unwell? (*to an adult*)
(j) Are you ill? (*to an adult*)

5 Learn the phrases in 'At the doctor's'.

(a) In answer to question 1, tell the doctor that you have a high temperature.
(b) In answer to question 2, tell him that your throat is sore.

6 Learn all the new words.

7 Answer the following questions.

(a) What is the tourist suffering from?
(b) Where does he go for help?
(c) What is he given?
(d) What instructions is he given?

8
(a) You have gone to the chemist's in France.
  (i) Say hello to the chemist.
  (ii) Tell him that you have a stomach upset.
  (iii) Ask him if he can prescribe anything.
  (iv) Ask him how much it costs.

(b) Here are the chemist's replies. He questions you carefully before recommending a treatment. Can you understand his questions?
  (i) Quel âge avez-vous?
  (ii) Avez-vous mal autre part?
  (iii) Avez-vous la diarrhée?
  (iv) Avez-vous des allergies?

Some intelligent guesswork should help you!

(c) When the chemist is satisfied that he can suggest a remedy, he might say . . .

'Voici des comprimés. Prenez un comprimé dans un verre d'eau toutes les quatre heures.'

(**un comprimé** a tablet)

Now say in English what the chemist has recommended.

9 You have had a lot of new words and expressions to learn in this unit. Revise them all before doing the revision test below.

Give the French for . . .

(a) an eye
(b) the eyes
(c) the foot
(d) the mouth
(e) an ear
(f) the leg
(g) the knee
(h) the nose
(i) the arm
(j) a shoulder
(k) I feel unwell.
(l) I am ill.
(m) It is necessary to consult a doctor.
(n) I have a headache.
(o) I have a stomach upset.
(p) How are you? (*to a friend*)
(q) How are you? (*to an adult who is not a relative*)
(r) I have sunburn.
(s) I have a temperature.
(t) I have a cold.

Unit 11

Le Syndicat d'Initiative/ L'Office de Tourisme
– The Tourist Information Office

In this unit you will learn:
(1) *how to write a formal letter in French requesting information;*
(2) *the various forms of the interrogative adjective 'quel';*
(3) *how to express need in French.*

If you are on holiday in France and you want to find out about one or more of the following, the best place to seek information is at the local 'Syndicat d'Initiative'. There is usually one in every town and they will be able to give you information about . . .

la ville et les environs (*m*)   the town and region
les hôtels   hotels in the town
les campings   campsites in the area
les visites (*f*)   places of interest to visit
les événements à venir (*m*)   coming events
les promenades (*f*)   walks
les films (*m*)   films
les pièces de théâtre (*f*)   plays
les spectacles (*m*)   shows
les festivals (*m*)   festivals
les sports (*m*)   sport
la location des voitures   car-hire
les spécialités de la région (*f*)   regional specialities

Writing for information

However, if you would like to have information about a certain region before visiting, it would be a good idea to write to the 'Syndicat d'Initiative' in the town of your choice asking for the information you require. If you do not know the address of the Syndicat d'Initiative, you can simply address the envelope to the

Syndicat d'Initiative/Office de Tourisme
(name of the town)
France.

Marc and Céline are going to spend a few days in Rennes with their parents. They have not been to the town before and would like to have some information about it before they arrive. Céline is writing to the Syndicat d'Initiative for information. She has a special reason for writing the letter as you will see in the next column.

Valréas, le 2 octobre

Céline GAVARIN
6 Place de la Poste,
84600 VALRÉAS

Monsieur le Directeur
du Syndicat d'Initiative
Rennes

Monsieur,
Je vous prie de m'envoyer des informations sur la ville de Rennes. Voulez-vous m'envoyer des brochures, une liste des hôtels et un plan de la ville, s'il vous plaît?
Je vous serais très obligée de m'envoyer l'adresse du zoo de Rennes. J'ai besoin des informations sur les animaux sauvages du zoo pour un travail de recherches que je prépare pour mon professeur de biologie.
Avec mes remerciements anticipés, je vous prie d'agréer, Monsieur, l'expression de mes sentiments distingués.

Céline Gavarin

New words and expressions

prier   to ask/request
je vous serais très obligé(e) . . .   I would be very obliged to you . . .
j'ai besoin   I need
sauvage   wild
un travail de recherches   a project
préparer   to prepare
la biologie   biology
avec mes remerciements anticipés   thanking you in advance
je vous prie d'agréer l'expression de mes sentiments distingués   Yours faithfully

Au Syndicat d'Initiative

Touriste: Bonjour, mademoiselle, je cherche des informations sur la ville de La Rochelle. Quels hôtels pouvez-vous recommander? Quelles visites guidées y a-t-il aujourd'hui?

Employée: Voici une liste des hôtels et la liste des visites guidées d'aujourd'hui.

Touriste: Merci, mademoiselle. Quel est le meilleur hotel de la ville, s'il vous plaît?

Employée: Le Yachtman est le meilleur hôtel.

Touriste: Dans quelle rue, s'il vous plaît?

Employée: Sur le quai Valin.

Touriste: Vous avez un plan de la ville?

Employée: Voilà, monsieur.

Touriste: Merci, mademoiselle.

New words

une visite guidée   a guided visit
le meilleur hôtel   the best hotel
le quai   the quay

'Quel'

In the conversation at the Tourist Information Office, you saw the following:

> **Quel** est le meilleur hôtel . . .?
> Dans **quelle** rue . . .?
> **Quels** hôtels . . .?
> **Quelles** visites . . .?

There are four different forms of the word 'which' in French when it is used as an interrogative adjective (i.e. with a noun to ask a question).

masc. sing.	**quel** hôtel?	Which hotel?
fem. sing.	**quelle** rue?	Which street?
masc. pl.	**quels** hôtels?	Which hotels?
fem. pl.	**quelles** visites?	Which visits?

You have already used some of these forms in Volume 1,

e.g.   **Quelle** heure est-il?
        What time is it?

Quel âge as-tu?
How old are you? (Literally, what age?)

So **quel(le)(s)** can also mean 'what'; but, they are always used with nouns.

'I need . . .'

In Unit 10 you learnt 'il faut' (It is necessary). If you wish to say 'I need', you can use . . .

> **il me faut . . .**

e.g.   **Il me faut** un plan de la ville.
        Il me faut une liste des hôtels.

or   **J'ai besoin de . . .**

e.g.   Céline wrote . . .
        J'ai besoin des informations sur les animaux sauvages.

Remember that 'de' will change depending on what follows. In the example above it became 'des'. It might change to 'd' . . .'

e.g.   J'ai besoin **d'**une liste des hôtels.

Unit 11 continued

Information from the Tourist Office

Here is an example of the kind of letter you might receive if you wrote to the Syndicat d'Initiative at La Rochelle.

New words

You have not yet learnt all the words which you can see in the letter but here are a few new and important ones.

votre courrier   means 'votre lettre'
les renseignements   means 'les informations'
le plaisir   pleasure
accueillir   to welcome
faciliter   to make easy
le séjour   stay (do you remember the other meaning in Volume 1?)

The Tourist Office is sending you the information requested and they hope that you will call there when you are in La Rochelle.

Can you see the way they have expressed the French for 'Yours faithfully'? This is a variation used by offices.

OFFICE DE TOURISME - SYNDICAT D'INITIATIVE DE LA ROCHELLE

10, rue Fleuriau - 17025 LA ROCHELLE CEDEX

La Rochelle, le ————————

Tél. (46) 41.14.68
C.C.P. BORDEAUX 558-56

Madame, Monsieur,

C'est avec plaisir que nous avons reçu votre courrier et que nous vous adressons la documentation et les renseignements souhaités.

Lors de votre visite en notre ville, nous serons heureux de vous accueillir à notre pavillon et de faciliter votre séjour.

Nous vous prions de croire, Madame, Monsieur, à l'expression de nos sentiments dévoués.

L'Equipe de l'Office du Tourisme.

Here is an extract from the information sent from the Syndicat d'Initiative in La Rochelle. With a knowledge of some key words, you will be surprised how much you can understand.

More new words

horaires   times/timetables
tarifs   entrance fee
sauf   except
entrée gratuite   entry free
Pâques   Easter
La Pentecôte   Whitsuntide

MONUMENTS MUSÉES ET CURIOSITÉS

MUSÉE D'ORBIGNY – rue St Côme
MUSÉE DES BEAUX ARTS – rue Gargoulleau – Tél. (46) 41 18 83

Horaires :
du 15 juin au 15 septembre   : de 10 h à 12 h et de 14 h à 18 h
du 15 septembre au 15 juin   : de 10 h à 12 h et de 14 h à 17 h

Ces deux musées sont ouverts toute l'année, sauf dimanche matin et mardi.
Le Musée des Beaux Arts ferme à 16 h (du 15 décembre au 15 avril).
Les billets sont valables pour les 2 musées.

Tarifs : Individuels : 3 F   Groupes : 1,50 F
Période d'exposition – Individuels : 5 F – Groupes : 2,50 F (par pers.)

MUSÉUM D'HISTOIRE NATURELLE
Rue Albert 1er – Tél. (46) 41 18 25

Horaires :
du 15 juin au 15 septembre   : de 10 h à 12 h et de 14 h à 18 h
du 15 septembre au 15 juin   : de 10 h à 12 h et de 14 h à 17 h
Ouvert toute l'année sauf dimanche matin et lundi.

Tarifs : Individuels : 3 F   Groupes : 1,50 F (par pers.)

MUSÉE OCÉANOGRAPHIQUE
Port des Minimes – Tél. (46) 45 17 87

Horaires :
du 1 er mai au 30 septembre   : 10 h 30 à 12 h 30 et 14 h 30 à 19 h
du 1 er octobre au 1 er mai   : 10 à 12 h et 14 h 17 h

(jusqu'à 18 h le samedi et le dimanche)

Fermé le dimanche matin et le samedi.
(Ouvert exceptionnellement les lundis de Pâques et de la Pentecôte.)

Tarifs : Individuels : 3 F   Groupes : 1,50 (par pers.)

MUSÉE DU NOUVEAU MONDE
10, rue Fleuriau – Tél. (46) 41 46 50

Horaires :
ouvert de 10 h 30 à 18 h 30 (sans interruption)
Fermé le mardi

Tarifs : Individuels : 5 F   Groupes : ½ tarif : 2,50 F

MUSÉE PROTESTANT
Rue Saint Michel (derrière l'Hôtel de Ville)

Horaires :
du 1 er juillet au 15 septembre   : de 14 h 30 à 18 h

(Le reste de l'année, demander à la conciergerie.)
Entrée gratuite.

TOUR DE LA LANTERNE DITE DES 4 SERGENTS
TOUR SAINT NICOLAS

– Tour de la Lanterne ou des ‹‹4 Sergents››

Horaires :
du 1 er avril au 30 septembre   : de 10 h à 12 h et de 14 h à 18 h 30
du 1 er octobre au 31 mars   : de 14 h à 17 h

– Tour Saint Nicolas

Horaires :
du 1 er avril au 30 septembre   : de 10 h à 12 h et de 14 h à 19 h
du 1 er octobre au 31 mars   : de 14 h à 17 h

Activités

1 Learn all the new words and expressions. Without looking at this book, see if you can write out the French expression for 'Yours faithfully'.

2 Answer the following questions in English.

(a) What three things does Céline ask the Tourist Office to send her at the beginning of the letter?

(b) What else does she ask them to send her?

(c) What information does she require in the second paragraph?

(d) What is she preparing?

(e) Who is she preparing it for?

3 Using Céline's letter as a model, write a letter to the Syndicat d'Initiative at La Rochelle (in your Record Book). Ask them for a list of hotels, a list of campsites and information about coming events. End your letter with the French expression for 'Yours faithfully'.

4 Learn the new words, then answer the following questions in English.

(a) What particular information does the tourist ask for at the beginning of the conversation?

(b) What specific information does he ask for about the hotels recommended?

(c) Which is the best hotel?

(d) In what part of the town is it?

(e) What does the tourist need to get there?

5 Put in the correct form of 'quel(le)(s)' in the following questions and then say what they mean in English.

(a) ..... sports?

(b) ..... événements à venir?

(c) .... promenades?

(d) ...... ville?

(e) ..... spectacles?

(f) .... film?

(g) ..... campings?

(h) .... spécialités de la région?

(i) .... travail de recherches?

(j) .... quai?

6 Give two different ways of saying in French . . .

(a) I need a plan of the town.

(b) I need information on the town of Rennes.

(c) I need some brochures.

(d) I need a list of restaurants.

(e) I need information on the coming events.

7 Learn the key words in the extract, then answer the questions below in English.

(a) At what time does the Musée d'Histoire Naturelle (the Natural History Museum) close for lunch from 15 June to 15 September?

(b) On which days (or parts of days) is it closed?

(c) What is the individual entrance fee for the Musée Océanographique (Oceanography Museum)?

(d) How much does it cost to go into the Musée Protestant (Protestant Museum)?

(e) On which day of the week is the Musée du Nouveau Monde (New World Museum) closed?

Unit 12

En voyage/ Travelling

In *this unit you will:*
(1) practise using the 24-hour clock;
(2) learn about public transport in France;
(3) learn how to ask for and give information about times of journeys;
(4) learn how to ask for and give information about distances in French;
(5) learn the verb 'partir' (to leave).

The 24-hour clock

At the end of Unit 11 you saw part of an extract from a tourist brochure. The times given in the brochure were based on the 24-hour clock. Here is a reminder for you of the 24-hour clock system.

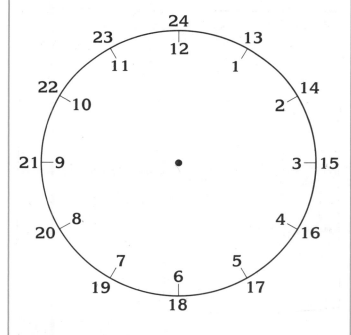

This system is used in France for road, rail, sea and air travel timetables.

Now learn the following words before attempting Activité 1.

New words

un autobus   bus
un avion   plane
un car   coach (N.B. do not mistake this French word for its English-sounding equivalent)

le ferry   ferry
l'hovercraft   hovercraft
le métro   underground railway
le mini-bus   minibus
le train   train
partir   to leave
à quelle heure part . . .   at what time does . . . leave?
le premier . . .   first
le dernier . . .   last
le prochain . . .   next
arriver   to arrive

Public transport in France

Here are some of the different ways one can travel in France using the public transport system.

En autobus – by bus (for journeys within a town)

(a) To catch the bus, wait at the **arrêt d'autobus** (bus stop).

(b) It is advisable to buy a **carnet de tickets** (book of tickets) as you may need a few for just one journey and it is cheaper than buying single tickets.

N.B. In Paris the same tickets are used by both buses and the **métro** (underground railway). Most people buy a 'carnet de tickets' beforehand from an automatic machine. Once you are on the bus you normally have to punch your ticket in the machine inside the bus to cancel it.

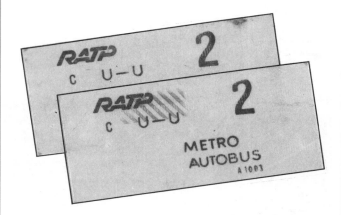

En avion – by plane
Most of the large provincial towns have domestic flights to and from Paris.

En car – by coach
(a) To get on a coach, go to **la gare routière** (coach station), or wait at the **arrêt d'autocar** (bus stop).

(b) Some coaches are run by the SNCF (French railways) to connect with rail services, and are called **cars en correspondance**.

En train – by train
You will learn more about travelling by train in the next unit and more about travelling on the underground in Volume 3.

Unit 12 *continued*

'Partir'

Here is the present tense of the verb **partir** (to leave).

je pars   I leave,
tu pars   etc.
il part
elle part
nous partons
vous partez
ils partent
elles partent

Dans la rue

Touriste: Pardon, monsieur, y a-t-il une gare routière près d'ici?

Passant: Oui, mademoiselle, à cent mètres, à droite.

Touriste: Merci, monsieur. Savez-vous s'il y a des cars pour Toulouse cet après-midi?

Passant: Oui, mademoiselle. Il y a un car à cinq heures.

Touriste: Merci, monsieur.

Passant: De rien.*

* **'Not at all'.**

In the conversation above, the tourist asks if there is a bus station nearby. You might need to ask if it is far, or perhaps how far it is. Here are some useful expressions.

C'est loin la gare routière?
(Is the bus station far?)

A quelle distance se trouve la gare routière?
(How far is the bus station?)

Use of 'à' in distances

When giving locations and distances in French, you should use 'à' in front of the number of metres or kilometres.

e.g.   La gare routière se trouve **à** cent metres d'ici.
       (The bus station is 100 metres from here.)

L'horaire des cars bleus

LIGNE 3 RÉMUZAT–AVIGNON

RÉMUZAT	06.15	12.15	18.15
NYONS	07.00	13.00	19.00
VALRÉAS	07.30	13.30	19.30
ORANGE	08.30	14.30	20.30
AVIGNON	09.15	15.15	21.15

N.B. **ligne**   route number

Une Agence de Voyages

Voici une Agence de Voyages. On peut retenir dans cette agence des billets pour les voyages à l'étranger. On peut y retenir les billets d'avion aussi, mais pour retenir les billets de train, on va d'habitude à la gare.

New words
une agence de voyages   travel agent's
retenir   to book

Activités

1 How would you ask for the following information in French?

e.g. At what time does the next train leave for Boulogne?

A quelle heure part le prochain train pour Boulogne?

(a) At what time does the next coach leave for Paris?

(b) At what time does the first bus leave for Vincennes?

(c) At what time does the last ferry leave?

(d) At what time does the next ferry leave?

(e) At what time does the next train arrive?

(f) At what time does the next plane arrive?

(g) At what time does the next hovercraft leave?

(h) At what time does the last train leave?

(i) At what time does the next train leave for Lyon?

(j) At what time does the minibus leave?

2 In answer to the questions above, you might hear the following answers. Say in English at what time in the morning, afternoon or evening they leave/arrive.

(a) Le prochain car pour Paris part à quatorze heures.

(b) Le premier autobus pour Vincennes part à cinq heures et demie.

(c) Le dernier ferry part à vingt-trois heures.

(d) Le prochain ferry part à onze heures et quart.

(e) Le prochain train arrive à seize heures.

(f) Le prochain avion arrive à quinze heures.

(g) Le prochain hovercraft part à dix-neuf heures.

(h) Le dernier train part à vingt-deux heures.

(i) Le prochain train pour Lyon part à dix heures et demie.

(j) Le mini-bus part à dix-huit heures.

3 Learn all the parts of the verb 'partir' carefully. Then complete the sentences below with the correct part of the verb.

(a) Le prochain car .... à dix heures.

(b) Nous .... à neuf heures et demie.

(c) Tu .... à huit heures?

(d) Elles .... à midi.

(e) Vous ...... à six heures?

(f) Le premier train .... à vingt heures.

(g) Il .... à vingt heures.

(h) Je .... pour Paris.

(i) Elle .... pour Lyon.

(j) Ils .... à cinq heures moins le quart.

4 Read the conversation aloud in French. Then answer the following questions in English.

(a) What information is the tourist seeking at the beginning of the conversation?

(b) How far away is it?

(c) In which direction?

(d) What is the second piece of information that the tourist asks for?

(e) What answer is she given?

5 Using 'C'est loin . . .?'
or 'A quelle distance se trouve . . .?',

whichever is the most appropriate, how would you ask in French?

(a) Is the station far?

(b) How far is the station, please?

(c) Is the bus stop far?

(d) How far is the bus stop, please?

(e) Is the airport far? (l'aéroport)

(f) How far is the airport, please?

(g) Is the hoverport far? (l'hoverport)

(h) How far is the hoverport, please?

(i) Is the metro station far? (la station de métro)

(j) How far is the metro station, please?

6 In answer to the questions in Activité 5, you might hear the following answers. Tell your parents in English what information you are given.

(a) Non, à cinquante mètres d'ici.

(b) A cinquante mètres d'ici.

(c) Non, à trente mètres d'ici.

(d) A trente mètres d'ici.

(e) Non, à deux kilomètres d'ici.

(f) A deux kilomètres d'ici.

(g) Non, à un kilomètre d'ici.

(h) A un kilomètre d'ici.

(i) Non, à cent mètres d'ici.

(j) A cent mètres d'ici.

7 Study the timetable for the Blue Coaches, then answer the following questions in French.

(a) A quelle heure part le premier car de Rémuzat?

(b) A quelle heure part le premier car de Nyons?

(c) A quelle heure part le dernier car de Nyons?

(d) A quelle heure part le dernier car d'Orange?

(e) A quelle heure part le premier car d'Orange?

(f) Le car de sept heures et demie de Valréas arrive à Avignon à quelle heure?

(g) Le car de treize heures trente de Valréas arrive à Avignon à quelle heure?

(h) Le car de dix-neuf heures trente de Valréas arrive à Avignon à quelle heure?

8 Write in English in your Record Book what information you are given about the photo of the travel agent's.

Unit 13

A la gare/
At the railway station

In this unit you will:
(1) be given information about French railways;
(2) learn how to buy tickets and book seats for French trains;
(3) learn about direct object pronouns.

La SNCF (La Société Nationale des Chemins de Fer Français) – the French Railways

When you go into a French railway station, one of the first signs you will see will be . . .

> ACCÈS AUX QUAIS
> To the trains

If you go to one of the large stations in Paris you will see that there are two sections:

> LES GRANDES LIGNES – main line trains
> and LES TRAINS DE BANLIEUE – suburban trains

The trains leave from platforms marked VOIE (with a number).

In this photo you can see **Voie 7** and **Voie 8**.

The times of arrival (**Arrivée**) and departure (**Départ**) of trains are given on large indicator boards. Here is an indicator board giving departure details of some suburban trains about midday.

Once inside the railway station you will notice other signs. Here are some of the important ones.

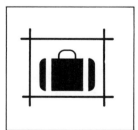

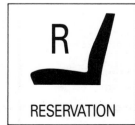

Au Bureau de Renseignements

Voyageur: Il y a un train pour Belfort cet après-midi, mademoiselle?

Employée: Oui, à quinze heures trente, monsieur.

Voyageur: C'est un train direct?

Employée: Non, monsieur, il faut changer à Dijon.

Voyageur: Et de quelle voie part le train pour Dijon, s'il vous plaît, mademoiselle?

Employée: Il part de la voie numéro sept, monsieur.

Voyageur: C'est où la voie sept, s'il vous plaît?

Employée: La voilà, à droite.

Voyageur: Faut-il réserver une place?

Employée: Non, monsieur.

Voyageur: Et les bagages? Où peut-on les laisser?

Employée: Vous pouvez les laisser à la consigne automatique.

Voyageur: C'est où . . .

Employée: A gauche, monsieur!

Voyageur: Merci, mademoiselle.

Employée: Je vous en prie, monsieur.

New words

un train direct a through train
changer to change
réserver to reserve
une place a place/seat
les bagages (*mpl*) luggage
laisser to leave

Unit 13 continued

Buying tickets

Here are two photos showing where you can buy tickets and reserve seats.

BILLETS BANLIEUE – suburban train tickets (from an automatic machine)

BILLETS GRANDES LIGNES – tickets for main line trains

BILLETS AVEC RÉSERVATIONS – ticket reservations

When you buy a train ticket you will be asked if you want . . .

	un aller simple	a single ticket
or	**un aller et retour**	a return ticket
	première classe	first class
or	**deuxième classe**	second class

Au guichet des billets

Voyageur: Un aller simple pour Nancy, s'il vous plaît.

Employé: De première ou de deuxième classe, monsieur?

Voyageur: De première classe et je voudrais réserver une place.

Employé: C'est pour aujourd'hui, monsieur?

Voyageur: Oui, pour le train de midi.

Employé: Le voilà, monsieur. Ça fait cent vingt francs.

Voyageur: Les voici.

Employé: Merci, monsieur.

Direct object pronouns

In the two conversations 'Au Bureau de Renseignements' and 'Au Guichet des Billets' you read the following sentences:

Le voilà.   There **it** is.   (*referring to 'le billet'*)

La voilà.   There **it** is.   (*referring to 'la voie'*)

Les voici.   Here **they** are.   (*referring to 120 francs*)

Vous pouvez **les** laisser à la consigne automatique.

You can leave **them** in the left luggage lockers. (*referring to 'les bagages'*)

'le'/'la'/'les' in the above sentences are all direct object pronouns. They refer to nouns which have already been mentioned.

N.B.   The position they occupy is *in front* (not after as in English)

But . . .

Le can also mean 'him'

La can also mean 'her'

Les can refer to people as well as to things.

Learn the following examples:

Je vois le train. Je **le** vois.	(I see it)
Je vois l'employé. Je **le** vois.	(I see him)
Je vois la gare. Je **la** vois.	(I see it)
Je vois l'employée. Je **la** vois.	(I see her)
Je vois les trains. Je **les** vois.	(I see them)
Je vois les voyageurs. Je **les** vois.	(I see them)

N.B.   **le** and **la** become **l'** in front of a vowel

J'achète le billet.   Je **l'**achète.

J'achète la robe.   Je **l'**achète.

Here are some more direct object pronouns:

me	(me)
te	(you)
nous	(us)
vous	(you)

e.g.   Il **me** voit.   He sees me.

Il **vous** voit.   He sees you.

Always remember to put them *in front* of the verb in a statement.

Additional information

COMPOSTER or
N'OUBLIEZ PAS DE COMPOSTER

This means that you must put your ticket through the orange-coloured machine at the station before getting on the train in order to validate the ticket. You will be fined if you travel without validating your ticket.

TAC – car sleeper train
TAJ – daytime motorail train
TEE – Trans-Europ-Express
TEN – Trans-Euro-Nuit (night train)
TGV – Train à grande vitesse (high speed train)

Marc is a keen train-spotter. See if you, too, can spot any of these trains when you are in France.

Activités

1 Learn all the new words.

2 Read the conversation at the information desk aloud in French. Then answer the following questions in English about it.

(a) Where does the traveller wish to go?
(b) At what time is the train?
(c) Is it a through train?
(d) Where will the traveller have to change?
(e) From which platform will the train leave?
(f) Where is it?
(g) Should the traveller reserve a seat?
(h) Where are the left luggage lockers?

3 You are at the information desk at a railway station. What would you say in French to ask for the following information?

(a) Is there a train for Bordeaux this morning?
(b) Is it a through train?
(c) From what platform does the train for Bordeaux leave?
(d) Is it necessary to reserve a seat?
(e) Where is the waiting-room, please?

4 Read the conversation aloud with a friend or with one of your parents.

5 Answer the following questions in English.

(a) Where does the traveller want to go?
(b) Does he want a single or return ticket?
(c) First or second class?
(d) What else does he require?
(e) On which day is he going to travel?
(f) At what time?
(g) How much does his ticket cost? (Give your answer in francs and then the English equivalent.)

6 You are at the booking-office of a French railway station. What would you say in French to ask for the following . . .?

(a) A single ticket for Paris, please.
(b) Second class.
(c) A return ticket for Paris, please.
(d) First class.
(e) I would like to reserve a seat.

7 Fill in the gaps in the second sentences with a direct object pronoun which replaces the word in heavy type in the first sentence.

e.g. J'achète **les billets.**
     Je les achète.

Remember to place the object pronoun *in front* of the verb.

(a) Il achète **les billets**.
    Il ... achète.
(b) Il achète **le billet**.
    Il .. achète.
(c) Je réserve **la place**.
    Je .. réserve.
(d) Nous réservons **les places**.
    Nous ... réservons.
(e) Nous voyons **l'employé**.
    Nous .. voyons.
(f) Elle attend **le prochain train**.
    Elle .. attend.
(g) Vous attendez **le prochain train**?
    Vous .. attendez?
(h) Voici **le train**.
    .. voici.
(i) Voilà **l'employée**.
    .. voilà.
(j) Voici **la gare**.
    .. voici.

8 How would you say in French . . .

(a) I see you (*to a friend*)
(b) I see you (*to several friends*)
(c) He sees us
(d) She sees us
(e) We see you (*to a group of people*)

Unit 14

A la douane/ Going through Customs

In this unit you will:
(1) be given information about going through French Customs;
(2) practise answering questions at the Customs;
(3) learn about indirect object pronouns;
(4) learn the verb 'ouvrir' (to open).

Here are some important words you will need to know about going through Customs in France.

un aéroport airport
l'alcool alcohol
un appareil-photo camera
le comptoir counter
la contrebande contraband
le contrôle des passeports passport-control
la Douane Customs

le douanier Customs officer
fixement intently
fumer to smoke
interroger to question
montrer to show
un objet de valeur valuable object
ouvrir to open
le parfum perfume
le passeport passport
le policier police officer
présenter les bagages to show one's luggage
le sac à dos rucksack
le sac à main handbag
seul alone
sortir to go out
la valise suitcase
le voyageur traveller
Avez-vous quelque chose à déclarer? Do you have anything to declare?
Je n'ai rien à déclarer I have nothing to declare

Passport control and Customs

When the Gavarin family went to England on holiday, they had to go through passport control and through Customs. When you go to France, you too will have to do the same. Here is some information for you about passport control and the Customs. Read it carefully so that you know what to expect.

Au contrôle des passeports

Quand vous arrivez en France, vous devez aller au contrôle des passeports. Il y a un contrôle des passeports et une douane à tous les ports et à tous les aéroports. Vous devez donner votre passeport au policier au contrôle des passeports. Il le regarde. Il regarde votre photo puis il vous regarde fixement. Quelquefois il vous interroge et vous devez lui répondre.

'Combien de temps allez-vous rester en France?'
'Voyagez-vous seul?'
Si tout va bien, vous pouvez passer . . .

À la douane

Là, il y a les douaniers derrière un long comptoir. Vous devez leur présenter vos bagages.

Douanier: Ce sont vos bagages?

Touriste: Oui, monsieur.

Douanier: Mettez-les sur le comptoir puis ouvrez-les. Avez-vous quelque chose à déclarer? De la contrebande?

Touriste: Non, monsieur je n'ai rien à déclarer.

Douanier: Vous avez des cigarettes, du parfum, de l'alcool?

Touriste: J'ai une petite bouteille de whisky. C'est un cadeau pour les parents de mon correspondant. Mes parents leur offrent la bouteille.

Douanier: Montrez-la-moi. (Le touriste lui montre la bouteille.)

Touriste: La voilà, monsieur.

Douanier: Vous avez des objets de valeur?

Touriste: Oui, j'ai un appareil-photo, mais il est vieux.

Douanier: Montrez-le-moi.

Touriste: Le voilà, monsieur.

Douanier: Vous avez des cigarettes?

Touriste: Non, monsieur, je ne fume pas.

Douanier: Bon. Vous pouvez sortir. Le prochain.

'Ouvrir'

Although the verb 'ouvrir' ends in '–ir', the present tense has the same endings as regular '–er' verbs.

Ouvrir   to open
j'ouvr**E**   I open,
tu ouvr**ES**   etc.
il ouvr**E**
elle ouvr**E**
nous ouvr**ONS**
vous ouvr**EZ**
ils ouvr**ENT**
elles ouvr**ENT**

Indirect object pronouns

In the passage about passport control and the Customs, you saw the following pronouns:

lui   (*to* him/*to* her)
leur   (*to* them)

e.g.   Le touriste **lui** montre la bouteille.
(. . . shows **to** him . . .)
Mes parents **leur** offrent la bouteille.
(. . . give **to** them . . .)

N.B.   these indirect pronouns are placed *in front* of the verb.

In the examples above,
lui is used instead of saying '**au** douanier'
leur is used instead of saying '**à** ses parents'

Extra note

'Lui' and 'leur' are also used with such verbs as 'dire' and 'demander' since you ask 'to' someone and tell 'to' someone . . .

e.g.   Je **lui** dis bonjour.
Je **leur** demande mon appareil-photo.

The pronouns **me**, **te**, **nous**, **vous** also mean **to** me/**to** you/**to** us/**to** you.

e.g.   Il **me** donne la valise.
Il **te** donne le passeport.
Il **nous** donne les billets.
Il **vous** offre une bouteille de whisky.

In all of the statements above, the object pronoun is placed *in front* of the verb, unlike English, *but* . . .
when you give an affirmative command in French the pronouns follow the verb and are joined to the verb with a hyphen (-)

e.g.   in the conversation earlier in this unit, you saw . . .
Mettez-les sur le comptoir.
(Put them on the counter.)

and   **Ouvrez-les**.
(Open them.)

and   **Montrez-la-moi**.
(Show it to me.)

The order of 'verb-pronoun' remains the same as in the English command. The direct object pronoun should go before the indirect object pronoun.

N.B.   'me' is changed to 'moi'
'te' is changed to 'toi' in affirmative commands.

Activités

1 Learn all the new words. Then give yourself a vocabulary test by covering up the left-hand words while you give the meanings aloud in French.

2 Did you understand what was being said in the conversation at the Customs and Passport Control? Answer the following questions in English.

(a) When you arrive at a French port, where do you have to go to first?
(b) When you arrive at a French airport, where do you have to go to first?
(c) What do you have to do there?
(d) What two questions might you be asked?
(e) Where do you have to go next?
(f) What do you have to do there?
(g) What in general is the officer looking for?
(h) What in particular does he ask about?
(i) What does the tourist say about the bottle of whisky?
(j) Why doesn't he have any cigarettes?

3 Learn the verb 'ouvrir', then complete the following sentences with the correct part of the present tense.

(a) Elle ..... la valise.
(b) Ils .... les passeports.
(c) J'..... mon passeport.
(d) Tu ...... ton sac à main.
(e) Vous ...... votre valise.
(f) Elles .... leurs valises.
(g) Elle ..... son sac à main.
(h) Il ..... son sac à dos.
(i) Nous .... nos valises.
(j) J'..... ma valise.

4 Fill in the gaps in the second sentences with 'lui' or 'leur' (whichever is the most appropriate) to replace the words underlined in the first sentences.

(a) Le touriste montre le passeport <u>au policier</u>.
Le touriste .. montre le passeport.
(b) Il montre la valise <u>au douanier</u>.
Il ... montre la valise.
(c) Elle montre ses valises <u>aux douaniers</u>.
Elle .... montre ses valises.
(d) Elle montre son passeport <u>au policier</u>.
Elle ... montre son passeport.
(e) Il offre une bouteille de whisky <u>à ses amis</u>.
Il .... offre une bouteille de whisky.

5 How would you express in French?
e.g. Put it on the counter. (*referring to 'la valise'*)
Mettez-la sur le comptoir.

(a) Put it on the counter. (*referring to 'le passeport'*)
(b) Put them on the counter. (*referring to 'les valises'*)
(c) Show it to me. (*referring to 'le sac à main'*)
(d) Show them to me. (*referring to 'les valises'*)
(e) Open it. (*referring to 'le sac à main'*)
(f) Open it. (*referring to 'la valise'*)

Do you remember how to give affirmative commands with reflexive verbs? Check back to Unit 4 in this Volume if you are unsure.

(g) Hurry up. (*to a friend*)
(h) Get up. (*to a friend*)
(i) Let's sit outside the café. (Use the correct part of 'se mettre')
(j) Let's write to each other.

6 You are at the passport control desk in France. The officer asks you the following questions. What would you say in French to give him the correct answers.

(a) Montrez-moi votre passeport.
(Say 'Here it is, sir'.)
(b) Quel âge avez-vous?
(Give your age in French.)
(c) Combien de temps allez-vous rester en France?
(Tell him 'Three weeks, sir'.)
(d) Où allez-vous rester?
(Tell him 'In (À) Royan'.)
(e) Chez qui?
(Tell him with (chez) your correspondent.)
(f) Voyagez-vous seul?
(Tell him 'Yes, sir'.)

7 You now have to go through Customs. What would you say in French to give the correct answers to the following questions?

(a) Bonjour, monsieur (mademoiselle). Où sont vos bagages?
(Tell him 'Here they are, sir'.)
(b) Quels bagages avez-vous?
(Tell him you have a suitcase and a rucksack.)
(c) Avez-vous quelque chose à déclarer?
(Tell him that you have nothing to declare.)
(d) Avez-vous de l'alcool?
(Tell him 'No, sir'.)
(e) Avez-vous des cigarettes et du parfum?
(Tell him that you do not have any cigarettes but that you have a small bottle of perfume and that it is a present for your correspondent's mother.)

Unit 15

Les pays et les nationalités/ Countries and nationalities

In this unit you will learn:
(1) the French names for various countries and nationalities;
(2) how to make comparisons in French;
(3) how to express superlatives in French.

La géographie

Au collège la matière favorite de Céline c'est la géographie. Elle a une amie qui habite maintenant au Canada. L'année prochaine elle espère rendre visite à son amie. En ce moment Céline étudie la carte du monde. Son amie lui dit que le Canada est le plus beau pays du monde, même plus beau que la France.

New words

l'Afrique (*f*) Africa
L'Amérique du Sud (*f*) South America
l'Australie (*f*) Australia
le Canada Canada
la Chine China
les États-Unis USA
la France France
l'Inde (*f*) India
le Japon Japan
la Nouvelle Zélande New Zealand
la Russie Russia
la matière subject
favori(te) favourite
la géographie geography
en ce moment at this moment
étudier to study
la carte map
le monde the world
le plus the most
même even

Voici la carte du monde

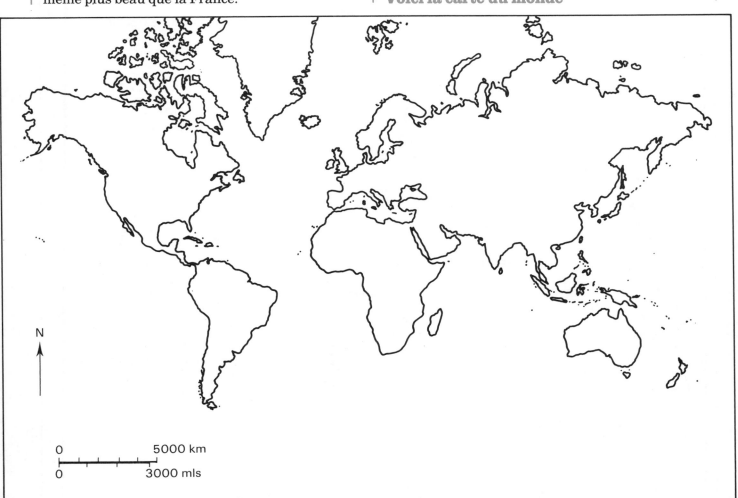

N

0   5000 km

0   3000 mls

Unit 15 continued

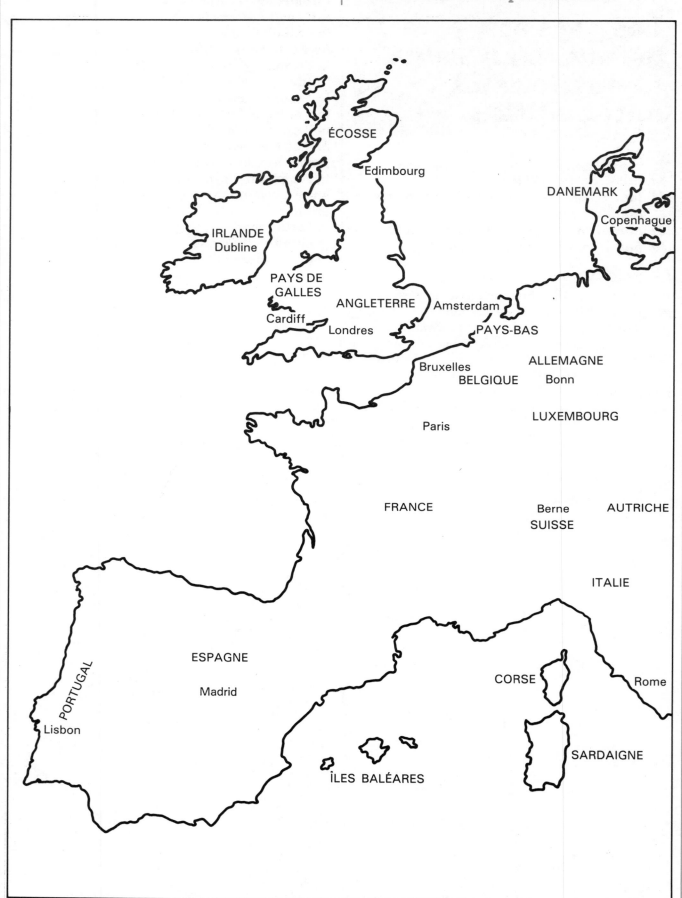

Les pays d'Europe occidentale

l'**Allemagne**   Germany
l'**Angleterre**   England
l'**Autriche**   Austria
la **Belgique**   Belgium
la **Corse**   Corsica
le **Danemark**   Denmark
l'**Écosse**   Scotland
l'**Espagne**   Spain
la **France**   France
les **Îles Baléares**   the Balearic Isles
l'**Irlande**   Ireland
l'**Italie**   Italy
le **Luxembourg**   Luxemburg
les **Pays-Bas**   the Netherlands
le **Pays de Galles**   Wales
le **Portugal**   Portugal
la **Sardaigne**   Sardinia
la **Suisse**   Switzerland

N.B.   all the countries in the above list with 'l"
   are feminine.

occidental(e)   western

Comparisons

(a) La France est **plus** grande **que** la Suisse.
(b) Le Luxembourg est **moins** grand **que** la
   Suisse.
(c) L'Autriche est **aussi** belle **que** la Suisse.

To make comparisons in French, use . . .

  plus . . . que   more . . . than . . .
moins . . . que   less . . . than . . .
  aussi . . . que   as . . . as . . .

N.B.   the adjective which comes in the middle of
   the comparison must agree with the first
   noun.

In (a) the adjective is feminine ('grand**e**') because
la France is feminine.

In (b) the adjective is masculine ('grand') because
le Luxembourg is masculine

In (c) the adjective is feminine ('belle') because
l'Autriche is feminine.

N.B.   to say 'not as . . . as . . .'
   use **ne . . . pas si . . . que**

e.g.   Le Danemark **n'**est **pas si** grand **que**
   L'Italie.

Les habitants

Un(e) Africain(e) habite l'**Afrique.**
Un(e) Anglais(e) habite l'**Angleterre.**
Un(e) Americain(e) habite l'**Amérique/les
   États-Unis.**
Un(e) Autrichien(ne) habite l'**Autriche.**
Un(e) Australien(ne) habite l'**Australie.**
Un(e) Belge habite la **Belgique.**

Un(e) Canadien(ne) habite le **Canada.**
Un(e) Chinois(e) habite la **Chine.**
Un(e) Corse habite la **Corse.**
Un(e) Danois(e) habite le **Danemark.**
Un(e) Ecossais(e) habite l'**Écosse.**
Un(e) Espagnol(e) habite l'**Espagne.**
Un(e) Français(e) habite la **France.**
Un(e) Indien(ne) habite l'**Inde.**
Un(e) Italien(ne) habite l'**Italie.**
Un(e) Japonais(e) habite le **Japon.**
Un(e) Luxembourgeois(e) habite le
   Luxembourg.
Un(e) Néozélandais(e) habite la **Nouvelle
   Zélande.**
Un(e) Néerlandais(e) habite les **Pays-Bas.**
Un(e) Gallois(e) habite le **Pays de Galles.**
Un(e) Portugais(e) habite le **Portugal.**
Un(e) Russe habite la **Russie.**
Un(e) Sarde habite la **Sardaigne.**
Un(e) Suisse(sse) habite la **Suisse.**

Superlatives (i.e. the most . . .)

Céline dit: 'La géographie est la matière **la plus**
   intéressante.'
Marc dit: 'La géographie est la matière **la plus**
   ennuyeuse.'
Céline lui dit: 'Tu es l'enfant **le plus** stupide.'
Marc lui répond: 'Je suis l'enfant **le plus**
   intelligent de ma classe.'
Céline dit: 'Quelle classe!'

To make an adjective superlative, put 'le plus' or
'la plus' in front of the adjective as shown above.
'Les plus' can also be used if the adjective refers to
a plural noun:

e.g.   **les plus** petits enfants   (the smallest
   children).

When using superlatives, take care to keep the
adjective in its normal position, i.e. before or after
the noun. Check back to Unit 13 in Volume 1 if
you need to revise the position of adjectives. 'le
plus'/'la plus'/'les plus' always come in front of the
adjective used (see the examples above).

N.B.   the comparative and superlative of
   bon(ne)(s) are . . .
   meilleur(e)(s)   better

e.g.   **un meilleur élève**   a better pupil

le(la) (les) meilleur(e)(s)   the best
e.g.   **la meilleure classe**   the best class

Some new adjectives

amusant   amusing
difficile   difficult
ennuyeux(se)   boring, tedious
facile   easy
intelligent   intelligent
jeune   young
stupide   stupid

Activités

1 Learn all the new words. Then answer the following questions in English.

(a) What is Céline's favourite subject at school?
(b) Where does her friend now live?
(c) What is Céline hoping to do next year?
(d) What is she doing at the moment?
(e) What does her friend think of Canada?
(f) How does this compare with France?

2 Learn all the new words in the list of countries in western Europe.

3 Marc is having problems with his geography homework. He doesn't have a map of western Europe. Can you help him?

e.g. Quelle est la capitale de l'Irlande?
    Dublin est la capitale de l'Irlande.

(a) Quelle est la capitale de l'Espagne?
(b) Quelle est la capitale de la Suisse?
(c) Quelle est la capitale de la Belgique?
(d) Quelle est la capitale de l'Écosse?
(e) Quelle est la capitale du Pays de Galles?
(f) Quelle est la capitale de l'Angleterre?
(g) Quelle est la capitale de l'Allemagne?
(h) Quelle est la capitale des Pays-Bas?
(i) Quelle est la capitale du Danemark?
(j) Quelle est la capitale de l'Italie?

4 Make the following comparisons in French. Remember to make the adjective agree with the first noun. Remember also to use the word 'the' in front of the name of the country.

e.g. France is bigger than England.
    La France est plus grande que l'Angleterre

(a) Canada is bigger than France.
(b) Japan is smaller than Russia.
(c) Wales is as green as Ireland.
(d) Portugal is less green than Scotland.
(e) Sardinia is as beautiful as Corsica.

5 Où habite-t-il/elle?

e.g. Un Japonais?   **Il habite le Japon**.
    Une Sarde?   **Elle habite la Sardaigne**.

(a) Une Écossaise?
(b) Un Irlandais?
(c) Un Espagnol?
(d) Une Néerlandaise?
(e) Une Belge?
(f) Une Danoise?
(g) Un Chinois?
(h) Un Luxembourgeois?
(i) Une Néozélandaise?
(j) Un Russe?

6 Learn the new adjectives, then complete the following sentences with the superlative of the given adjective

e.g. Marc est l'enfant......... (intelligent).
    Marc est l'enfant **le plus** intelligent.

(a) La géographie est la matière...... (facile).
(b) La biologie est la matière... (difficile).
(c) Marc et Céline sont les enfants... (intelligents).
(d) Marc est l'enfant ... (amusant).
(e) Quelquefois c'est l'enfant ... (ennuyeux).
(f) Marc est .... élève de sa classe. (jeune)
(g) La France est...... pays d'Europe. (beau)
(h) La Corse est ..... île de la Méditerranée. (belle)
(i) Céline est....élève de sa classe. (meilleure)
(j) Frédéric est ... élève de sa classe. (meilleux)

7 **A votre avis/In your opinion**
Answer the following questions in French.

(a) La géographie est plus/moins difficile que le français?
(b) La biologie est plus/moins difficile que le latin?
(c) Les filles sont plus/moins intelligentes que les garçons?
(d) Les garçons sont plus amusants que les filles?
(e) Les professeurs sont plus sévères que les parents?
(f) L'Angleterre est le plus beau pays?
(g) Londres est la capitale la plus intéressante?
(h) La Russie est le pays le plus important?
(i) Tu es le(la) plus grand(e) élève de ta classe?
(j) Tu es l'élève le(la) plus intelligent(e) de ta classe?

Unit 16

Un accident de la rue/ A street accident

In this unit you will learn:
(1) what to say and do in case of an accident in France;
(2) vocabulary for various problems that may occur;
(3) the verbs 's'asseoir' (to sit down) and 'être assis' (to be sitting down).

Un accident

Céline: Oh, regarde cet enfant-là. Il est assis au bord du trottoir et il pleure. Qu'est-ce qu'il a?

Marc et Céline s'approchent de l'enfant.

Céline: Qu'est-ce que tu as, mon petit? Ne pleure pas.

Le petit garçon: Oh...mon pied me fait mal. Un cycliste m'a renversé*. Je ne peux pas marcher.

Céline: Ne t'inquiète pas. Il y a un poste de police au coin de la rue. Mon frère va chercher un agent. Va vite, Marc, chercher un agent au poste. Il est dangereux d'être assis au bord du trottoir. Asseyons-nous sur ce banc. Je vais t'aider.

* **This is a new tense which you will learn how to use in the next unit. It is telling you what has happened.**

N.B. The verb 'avoir' is used to ask someone what is the matter. You are really saying 'What have you/they/etc?' You may also use the general expression **Qu'est-ce qu'il y a?** to ask 'What is the matter?'

Unit 16 continued

New words

assis sitting
au bord de at the edge
le trottoir pavement
pleurer to cry
Qu'est-ce qu'il a? What is the matter with him?
s'approcher de to approach
faire mal to hurt
le cycliste cyclist
renverser to knock over
marcher to walk
s'inquiéter to worry
le poste de police police-station
le coin the corner
dangereux dangerous
asseyons-nous let's sit down

A l'hôpital

Infirmière: Bonjour, les enfants. Qu'est-ce qu'il y a? (Elle remarque le petit garçon) Oh! Tu as mal au pied. Assieds-toi là.

Le petit garçon s'assied sur une chaise. Céline et Marc s'asseyent à côté de lui. L'infirmière regarde bien le pied blessé.

Infirmière: Je vais appeler un médecin pour le soigner.
Céline: Et moi, je vais téléphoner à la maman du petit pour lui dire où il est.
Infirmière: D'accord.

New words

une infirmière nurse
remarquer to notice
blessé injured
soigner to attend to/look after
d'accord all right/agreed

'S'asseoir'

In the conversation at the hospital, you read part of the verb 's'asseoir' (to sit down). This reflexive verb is irregular and you will need to learn the parts of the present tense carefully.

s'asseoir

je m'assieds I sit down,
tu t'assieds   etc.
il s'assied
elle s'assied
nous nous asseyons
vous vous asseyez
ils s'asseyent
elles s'asseyent

Imperative

Assieds-toi Sit down
Asseyons-nous Let us sit down
Asseyez-vous Sit down

In the first conversation in this unit you saw **il est assis** (he is sitting down). This verb 'être assis' describes the position someone is in. The verb 's'asseoir' above tells us what movement someone makes, i.e. going from a standing position to a sitting position.

e.g. elle s'assied   she sits down
elle est assise   she is sitting down
('assis' is treated like an adjective and therefore agrees with the subject)

Au secours:–Help!

Do you remember what to shout for 'Help' (Volume 1 Unit 23)?

Here are some more useful expressions to call in time of need. . .

Au feu!   Fire!
Au voleur!   Stop thief!
Attention!   Look out!

If you and your family are involved in an accident in France, you may be asked for. . .

votre nom et votre adresse your name and address

votre permis de conduire your (parents') driving-licence.

votre compagnie d'assurance your insurance company

votre carte internationale d'assurance automobile the Green Card required when motoring abroad.

In an emergency in France, you may need to use the phone. Can you remember the details about phoning in France that you were given in Unit 6 in this Volume? Here are some useful numbers for you:

(La) POLICE – 17
(Les) POMPIERS – 18   (fire brigade).

In France it is the 'pompiers' who deal with accidents and run the ambulance service.

Unit 16 continued

Injuries

You have already learnt the parts of the body in French. Here are some of the injuries which might occur.

blessé   wounded/injured
brûlé   burnt
cassé   broken
coupé   cut
foulé   sprained

Use these words as adjectives in Activité 9, i.e. add an 'e' and/or 's' if the part of the body is feminine and/or plural. Remember to put the adjective *after* the noun.

Activités

1 Learn all the new words. Then answer the following questions in English.

(a) Where is the little boy sitting?
(b) What is wrong with him?
(c) What does Céline say is nearby?
(d) What is Marc going to do?
(e) What is Céline going to do?

2 (a) What did Céline say in French when she asked 'What is the matter with him?'
(b) What did she say in French when she asked 'What is the matter with you?'

How would you ask in French . . .
(c) 'What is the matter with her?'
(d) 'What is the matter with them?'
(e) 'What is the matter?'

The little boy told Céline that his foot hurt. He said 'Mon pied **me fait mal**'. In Unit 10 you learnt another way of saying where you hurt. Can you remember it?

3 Give two ways of saying the following in French.

(a) My leg hurts.
(b) My head hurts
(c) My ear hurts.
(d) My knee hurts.
(e) My arm hurts.

4 Céline told Marc to go and get a policeman. She said 'Va chercher un agent'. If you were speaking to an adult you would say 'Allez chercher un agent'.

What would you say in French to the following people?

(a) Go and get my teacher. (*to a child*)
(b) Go and get my mother. (*to a child*)
(c) Go and get my father. (*to an adult*)
(d) Go and get a policeman. (*to an adult*)
(e) Go and get a doctor. (*to an adult*)

5 Learn the new words. Then answer the following questions in English.

(a) Where does the little boy sit?
(b) Where do Céline and Marc sit?
(c) What does the nurse look at?
(d) What is the nurse going to do?
(e) What is Céline going to do?

6 Give the French for . . .

(a) I sit down.
(b) I am sitting down.
(c) They (*fem.*) are sitting down.
(d) They (*masc.*) sit down.
(e) He sits down.
(f) She is sitting down.
(g) We sit down.
(h) Let us sit down.
(i) Sit down. (*to a friend*)
(j) Sit down. (*to a group of friends*)

7 There has been an accident. What would you say in French for . . .?

(a) What is the matter?
(b) We must call the police. (Use 'Il faut. . .')
(c) We must call a doctor.
(d) We must call an ambulance. (**une ambulance**)
(e) Help!

8 There has been an accident and you hear the following. What is being said?

(a) Au feu!
(b) Il faut appeler les pompiers.
(c) Il y a un enfant blessé.
(d) Il faut téléphoner à l'hôpital.
(e) Votre nom et votre adresse, s'il vous plaît.

9 How would you say in French . . .?
e.g.   the injured hand
      la main blessée

(a) the injured foot
(b) the injured head
(c) the burnt hands
(d) the burnt feet
(e) the broken wrist
(f) the broken leg
(g) the cut finger
(h) the cut nose
(i) the sprained wrist
(j) the sprained ankle.

Unit 17

Samedi dernier/
Last Saturday

In this unit you will:
(1) learn the 'perfect' tense of regular verbs using 'avoir';
(2) practise using the 'perfect' tense;
(3) learn the pronoun 'y' (there).

The 'perfect' tense

In Unit 16 the little boy told Céline what accident had happened to him. He said . . .

Un cycliste m' **a renversé**.
(A cyclist **knocked** me **over**.)

When you wish to tell someone what has happened in the past (whether it was a few seconds/minutes/hours/days/years ago) you should use the 'perfect' tense. It is called 'perfect' because the events are finished/completed.

There are two ways of forming the 'perfect' tense. In this Unit we shall look at regular verbs ending in '-er', '-ir', '-re', which use the verb 'avoir'. The **perfect tense** of these verbs is formed with the present tense of **avoir** and the **past participle** of the verb.

Type 1 '-er' verbs

e.g. 'regarder'

To form the past participle, the -r is removed from the infinitive and an acute accent (´) is added to the 'é', e.g. **regardé**.

The perfect tense of the verb **regarder** . . .

j'ai regardé I looked at/I have looked at
tu as regardé you looked at/you have looked at
il a regardé he looked at/he has looked at
elle a regardé she looked at/she has looked at
nous avons regardé we looked at/we have looked at
vous avez regardé you looked at/you have looked at
ils ont regardé they (*m*) looked at/they have looked at
elles ont regardé they (*f*) looked at/they have looked at

Type 2 '-ir' verbs

e.g. 'finir'

To form the past participle, the 'r' is removed – **fini**

The perfect tense of the verb **finir** . . .

j'ai fini I finished/I have finished
tu as fini you finished/you have finished
il a fini he finished/he has finished
elle a fini she finished/she has finished
nous avons fini we finished/we have finished
vous avez fini you finished/you have finished
ils ont fini they (*m*) finished/they have finished
elles ont fini they (*f*) finished/they have finished

Type 3 '-re' verbs

e.g. 'attendre'

To form the past participle, the '-re' is replaced by 'u' – **attendu**

The perfect tense of the verb '**attendre**'

j'ai attendu I waited/I have waited
tu as attendu you waited/you have waited
il a attendu he waited/he has waited
elle a attendu she waited/she has waited
nous avons attendu we waited/we have waited
vous avez attendu you waited/you have waited
ils ont attendu they (*m*) waited/they have waited
elles ont attendu they (*f*) waited/they have waited

N.B. Regular '-er', '-ir', 're' verbs will follow the patterns given above.

Le samedi dernier

Samedi dernier Madame Gavarin et Céline ont décidé d'aller en ville pour faire des courses. Elles y vont souvent mais il y a toujours beaucoup de monde en ville le samedi. Elles ont attendu l'autobus au coin de la rue. Elles y ont rencontré leurs voisines Madame Gérard et sa fille Marie-Christine. Céline et Marie-Christine sont dans la même classe au collège Pasteur.

En ville Madame Gavarin et Céline ont marché le long de la rue du Commerce. Elles ont regardé les vitrines de tous les magasins. Céline a aimé les robes dans les boutiques mais Madame Gavarin a préféré regarder les rayons de vêtements aux grands magasins.

Madame Gavarin: Dépêche-toi Céline. J'ai beaucoup à faire. Je ne peux pas m'arrêter tout le temps pour regarder toutes ces robes qui sont si chères.

Céline (devant une boutique): Oh, maman, entrons-y. Qu'elles sont jolies ces robes!

Madame Gavarin: Mais non, je n'ai pas fini de faire mes courses. Nous devons aller au supermarché là-bas.

Céline: Je déteste y faire des courses. Il y a tellement de monde. La semaine dernière j'y ai perdu mon porte-monnaie. Une dame a renversé son chariot. J'ai aidé la dame à ramasser ses provisions mais j'ai laissé tomber mon sac à main et quelqu'un a volé mon porte-monnaie. J'ai averti la police mais on n'a pas trouvé mon porte-monnaie.

Madame Gavarin: Combien d'argent as-tu perdu?

Céline: Quatre-vingts francs. Je regrette mais j'ai oublié de te le dire.

New words

décider to decide
le(la) voisin(e) neighbour
même same
le long de along
le porte-monnaie purse
les provisions (*fpl*) groceries
laisser tomber to drop
quelqu'un someone

The pronoun 'y'

The pronoun 'y' means 'there'. It is placed . . .

(1) in front of the verb in a statement,
    e.g. Elles **y** vont souvent.
    (They go there often.)

(2) in front of 'avoir' in the perfect tense,
    e.g. J'**y** ai perdu mon porte-monnaie
    (I lost my purse there.)

(3) (if there are two verbs together) in front of the verb it goes with,
    e.g. Je déteste **y** faire des courses.
    (I detest shopping there.)

(4) after the verb in a positive command.
    e.g. Entrons-**y**.
    (Let us go in there.)

N.B. If the 'tu' form command of the verb 'aller' is used, the 's' is retained with 'y'
i.e. **Vas-y!** (Go there.)

Activités

1 Give the 'je'/'vous'/'ils' forms of the perfect tense of. . .

(a) marcher   **(f)** choisir
(b) traverser   **(g)** avertir
(c) acheter   **(h)** vendre
(d) visiter   **(i)** rencontrer
(e) oublier   **(j)** répondre

2 Now give the English meanings for the answers to Activité 1.

3 Read the passage and conversation.

4 Learn the new words. Then answer the following questions by choosing which answer is the most appropriate.

(a) When did Madame Gavarin and Céline go to town?
   (i) last Monday
   (ii) last Tuesday
   (iii) last Friday
   (iv) last Saturday

(b) They go to town together . . .
   (i) rarely
   (ii) often
   (iii) every day
   (iv) every Wednesday

(c) Whom did they meet at the bus-stop?
   (i) their cousins
   (ii) their neighbour and her son
   (iii) their neighbour and her daughter
   (iv) some schoolfriends

(d) What kind of shop does Céline like looking at?
   (i) small dress shops
   (ii) department stores
   (iii) supermarkets
   (iv) record shops

(e) What does Madame Gavarin think about this kind of shop?
   (i) There isn't much choice.
   (ii) They are too crowded.
   (iii) They are too expensive.
   (iv) The goods are shoddy.

(f) What does Céline think about the supermarket?
   (i) It is too hot.
   (ii) It is too expensive.
   (iii) It is too noisy.
   (iv) It is too crowded.

(g) What happened when Céline was at the supermarket last week?
   (i) She knocked over a trolley.
   (ii) She broke a trolley.
   (iii) A woman knocked Céline over.
   (iv) A woman knocked a trolley over.

(h) Someone stole Céline's . . .
   (i) purse
   (ii) bag
   (iii) watch
   (iv) shopping

(i) Céline . . .
   (i) called the police.
   (ii) notified the police.
   (iii) shouted for the police.
   (iv) sent for the police.

(j) What did she lose?
   (i) 80 francs
   (ii) 24 francs
   (iii) everything
   (iv) nothing

5 Replace the words underlined with the pronoun 'y' and place in the correct position.

e.g.   Je vais <u>à la pharmacie</u>.
J'**y** vais
J'ai perdu mon sac à main <u>au supermarché</u>.
J'**y** ai perdu mon sac à main.
J'aime faire des courses <u>au supermarché</u>.
J'aime **y** faire des courses.
Allons <u>à la charcuterie</u>.
Allons-**y**.

(a) Je vais <u>à la boulangerie</u>.
(b) Nous allons <u>à la maison de la presse</u>.
(c) Elle a perdu son porte-monnaie <u>au supermarché</u>.
(d) Allons <u>à la boucherie</u>.
(e) Allez <u>à la pâtisserie</u>.
(f) J'aime aller <u>à la pâtisserie</u>.
(g) Elle aime faire ses courses <u>au supermarché</u>.
(h) J'ai perdu mon porte-monnaie <u>à la pharmacie</u>.
(i) Allez <u>à la boulangerie</u>.
(j) Elles vont <u>au rayon des vêtements</u>.

6 Change the verbs underlined in the following passage from the present tense to the perfect tense.

<u>Je décide</u> d'aller en ville pour faire des courses. <u>J'attends</u> l'autobus au coin de la rue. <u>J'y rencontre</u> mes amis. <u>Nous marchons</u> le long de la rue du Commerce. <u>Nous regardons</u> les vitrines des grands magasins. <u>Je préfère</u> les petites boutiques mais mes amis <u>préfèrent</u> les grands magasins. <u>J'achète</u> des provisions pour ma mère mais <u>je laisse</u> tomber mon sac à main. Mon ami Paul <u>ramasse</u> mon porte-monnaie.

Unit 18

Au supermarché/ At the supermarket

In this unit you will:
(1) learn the perfect tense of irregular verbs using 'avoir';
(2) practise using the perfect tense;
(3) learn the pronoun 'en'.

The perfect tense: irregular verbs

In Unit 17 you learnt the perfect tense of regular verbs with 'avoir'. Here are some of the irregular verbs which are conjugated with 'avoir' in the perfect tense. You must learn the past participles carefully.

avoir	–j'ai **eu**	I had, I have had
être	–j'ai **été**	I was, I have been
dire	–j'ai **dit**	I said, I have said

écrire	–j'ai **écrit**	I wrote, I have written
faire	–j'ai **fait**	I made (did), I have made (done)
vouloir	–j'ai **voulu**	I wanted (wished), I have wanted (wished)
voir	–j'ai **vu**	I saw, I have seen
devoir	–j'ai **dû**	I had to/owed, I have had to/have owed
pouvoir	–j'ai **pu**	I was able, I have been able
savoir	–j'ai **su**	I knew, I have known
mettre	–j'ai **mis**	I put, I have put
prendre	–j'ai **pris**	I took, I have taken
comprendre	–j'ai **compris**	I understood, I have understood

Here is the completed perfect tense of

voir (to see)
j'ai vu I saw, etc.
tu as vu
il a vu
elle a vu
nous avons vu
vous avez vu
ils ont vu
elles ont vu

Unit 18 continued

Au supermarché

Mercredi dernier Madame Gavarin a acheté des provisions au supermarché en ville. Dans le supermarché elle a pris un chariot qu'elle a poussé entre les rayons. D'abord elle a choisi des légumes. La famille Gavarin aime bien manger et Madame Gavarin prépare ses repas avec soin. Elle aime choisir des légumes frais mais quelquefois elle achète des boîtes de conserves. Elle a fait le tour du rayon des conserves et a pris quelques pots de confiture – confiture d'abricot et de framboise. Elle n'a pas pu trouver sa confiture favorite – la confiture de groseille. Elle en a demandé à la vendeuse qui lui a indiqué le rayon à gauche. Madame Gavarin a tout mis dans son chariot. Puis tout à coup elle a vu sa voisine, Madame Gérard, devant le rayon des fromages. Elles ont parlé des prix des fromages puis les deux dames ont continué à faire leurs achats ensemble. Madame Gavarin a écrit une liste mais Madame Gérard a oublié d'en écrire une. Elle n'a pas pu se rappeler ce que son mari lui a demandé d'acheter.

'Je dois téléphoner à mon mari pour lui demander ce qu'il m'a dit d'acheter. Je suis vraiment distraite!' a dit Madame Gérard.

'Moi aussi,' a répondu Madame Gavarin. 'Ce matin j'ai mis mes pantoufles pour sortir! Mon mari n'a pas voulu m'accompagner. Il sait que j'ai beaucoup à faire mais il déteste faire des courses. Je ne peux pas décider ce que nous allons manger ce soir. Hier nous avons mangé du porc, mais les enfants préfèrent le bifteck.'

New words

entre between
avec soin carefully
les boîtes de conserves tinned food
abricot apricot
framboise raspberry
groseille redcurrant
indiquer to point out
continuer to continue
la liste list
se rappeler to remember
vraiment really
distrait(e) absent-minded
les pantoufles (*fpl*) slippers
accompagner to accompany
le bifteck steak

The pronoun 'en'

In the passage in this unit you read the following . . .

Elle **en** a demandé à la vendeuse.
(She asked the shop-assistant for **some**.)

Madame Gérard a oublié **d'en** écrire une.
(Mrs Gérard has forgotten to write one **of them**.)

In statements and questions 'en' is always placed in front of the verb it goes with and it means 'some', 'of it', 'of them'. *But* remember that it is a pronoun and *cannot* be used with a noun. The word for 'some' when used with a noun is **des** e.g. **des légumes** some vegetables

Here are some more examples of the use of the pronoun 'en':

As-tu acheté des pommes de terre? – Oui, j'**EN** ai acheté un kilo.
(. . . I have bought a kilo **of them**)

As-tu acheté des yaourts? – Oui, j'**EN** ai acheté.
(. . . Yes, I have bought **some**.)

A la caisse/At the check-out

As you can see, the check-out in the supermarket is very familiar. When you pay at the check-out, you will be able to see the bill total on the machine, but listen carefully when the assistant tells you the total in French. See if you can understand what she is saying without looking at the till first.

Activités

1 Learn the past participles of the irregular verbs. Then complete the sentences below giving the correct form of the perfect tense.

(a) Elles (faire) des achats.
(b) Nous (dire) bonjour.
(c) Ils (vouloir) aller en ville.
(d) Je (prendre) le chariot.
(e) Vous (mettre) les provisions dans le panier.
(f) Il (avoir) un accident.
(g) Elle (écrire) une liste.
(h) Tu (pouvoir) porter toutes les provisions?
(i) Je (comprendre).
(j) Nous (voir) nos amis.

2 Read the passage carefully and learn all the new words. Then answer the following questions in French.

(a) Quand Madame Gavarin a-t-elle fait ses achats?
(b) Où a-t-elle fait ses achats?
(c) Qu'est-ce qu'elle a poussé entre les rayons du supermarché?
(d) Qui aime bien manger?
(e) Qu'est-ce que Madame Gavarin n'a pas pu trouver d'abord?
(f) Qui a indiqué le rayon à gauche?
(g) Comment s'appelle la voisine de Madame Gavarin?
(h) Devant quel rayon a-t-elle rencontré Madame Gérard?
(i) Qui a oublié d'écrire une liste?
(j) Qu'est-ce que Madame Gérard doit faire?
(k) Pourquoi?
(l) Qui est distraite?
(m) Qui est distraite aussi?
(n) Qu'est-ce que Madame Gavarin a mis ce matin pour sortir?
(o) Qui n'a pas voulu l'accompagner?
(p) Qui a beaucoup à faire?
(q) Qui déteste faire les achats?
(r) Qu'est-ce que Madame Gavarin ne peut pas décider?
(s) Qu'est-ce que la famille Gavarin a mangé hier?
(t) Qu'est-ce que les enfants préfèrent?

3 Tell your French friend that you wanted to buy the following articles in town.

e.g. a book
   J'ai voulu acheter un livre.

(a) a note-book
(b) a rubber
(c) a pen
(d) an exercise book
(e) a record (un disque)

(check the vocabulary in Volume 1 if you have forgotten these words)

4 But you had to buy the following for your mother.

e.g. **J'au dû acheter** des légumes pour ma mère.

(a) some pork
(b) some cheese
(c) some tinned food
(d) some bread
(e) a kilo of potatoes (pommes de terre)

5 Tell your French friend whom you saw there.

e.g. your father
   J'y ai vu mon père.

(a) your teacher
(b) your friend
(c) your sister
(d) the doctor
(e) your cousin(girl)

6 Madame Gavarin asks you if you have bought the following. Give an affirmative answer each time.

e.g. As-tu acheté des allumettes?
   Oui, j'en ai acheté.

   As-tu acheté des pommes?   (4)
   Oui, j'en ai acheté quatre.

(a) As-tu acheté des artichauts?
(b) As-tu acheté du beurre?
(c) As-tu acheté des cartes postales?
(d) As-tu acheté des cerises?
(e) As-tu acheté du pain?
(f) As-tu acheté des choux-fleurs?   (2)
(g) As-tu acheté des livres?   (3)
(h) As-tu acheté des carottes?   (Un kilo)
(i) As-tu acheté des fraises?   (Un demi-kilo)
(j) As-tu acheté du jambon?   (deux cents grammes)

7 Your bill at the check-out comes to the following amounts. Tell your parents in English how many francs/centimes they have to pay.

(a) cent soixante-deux francs quinze
(b) quatre-vingt-dix-sept francs vingt
(c) soixante-seize francs soixante-dix-huit
(d) deux cent quarante-neuf francs douze
(e) cinquante-trois francs quatre-vingt-onze

Unit 19

Les passe-temps/ Pastimes

In this unit you will learn:
(1) how to speak about hobbies in French;
(2) how to write to a penfriend telling him/ her about your hobbies/pastimes and what you did last week(end);
(3) the negative perfect tense.

Quel est ton passe-temps préféré?

Tu aimes les sports?

Unit 19 continued

Hier soir Monsieur Gavarin a bricolé.
Il n'a pas fait le jardinage.

Madame Gavarin a tricoté.
Elle n'a pas regardé la télévision.

Céline a fait ses devoirs.
Elle n'a pas regardé la télévision.

Marc a regardé la télévision.
Il n'a pas fait ses devoirs.

New words

construire   to make/construct
les maquettes (*fpl*)   models (small)
hier   yesterday
bricoler   to do do-it-yourself jobs
faire le jardinage   to do the gardening
tricoter   to knit

Tu aimes les animaux?

Tu collectionnes les timbres-poste?

81

Tu construis des maquettes?

Tu bricoles?

The perfect tense: negative form

When you want to use the negative form of the perfect tense, 'ne . . . pas' are used around 'avoir', (the auxiliary verb) and the past participle is placed at the end. Since 'avoir' begins with a vowel 'ne' becomes 'n' '.

e.g.   the negative perfect tense of 'regarder' . . .

je **n'**ai **pas** regardé   I did not look at/I have not looked at, etc.

tu **n'** as **pas** regardé
il **n'**a **pas** regardé
elle **n'**a **pas** regardé
nous **n'**avons **pas** regardé
vous **n'**avez **pas** regardé
ils **n'**ont **pas** regardé
elles **n'**ont **pas** regardé

The negative perfect tense of 'finir' . . .

je **n'**ai **pas** fini   I did not finish/I have not finished, etc.

tu **n'**as **pas** fini
il **n'**a **pas** fini
elle **n'**a **pas** fini
nous **n'**avons **pas** fini
vous **n'**avez **pas** fini
ils **n'**ont **pas** fini
elles **n'**ont **pas** fini

82

Unit 19 continued

The negative perfect tense of 'attendre' . . .

je **n**'ai **pas** attendu   I did not wait for/I have not waited for, etc.

tu **n**'as **pas** attendu
il **n**' a **pas** attendu
elle **n**'a **pas** attendu
nous **n**'avons **pas** attendu
vous **n**'avez **pas** attendu
ils **n**'ont **pas** attendu
elles **n**'ont **pas** attendu

Here is the first person negative perfect tense of some of the irregular verbs you have learnt . . .

je **n**'ai **pas** eu   I have not had/I didn't have
je **n**'ai **pas** été   I have not been/I wasn't
je **n**'ai **pas** dit   I have not said/I didn't say
je **n**'ai **pas** écrit   I have not written/I didn't write
je **n**'ai **pas** fait   I have not done(made)/I didn't do (make)
je **n**'ai **pas** vu   I have not seen/I didn't see
je **n**'ai **pas** pu   I have not been able/I wasn't able
je **n**'ai **pas** voulu   I have not wanted/I didn't want
je **n**'ai **pas** mis   I have not put/I didn't put
je **n**'ai **pas** pris   I have not taken/I didn't take

New words
Here are some more things you might do in your spare time.
aller au centre sportif   go to the sports centre
aller au club des jeunes   go to the youth club
coudre   to sew
danser   to dance
faire de l'aérobic   to do aerobics
faire du judo   to do judo
écouter des disques   listen to records
lire   read
nager   swim
patiner   skate
promener le chien   take the dog for a walk

Here are some useful verbs to use when telling someone what you like doing in your spare time . . .
Je suis amateur de . . .   I am fond of ../like . . .
J'adore . . .
J'aime . . .
Je préfère . . .
Je collectionne . . .
Je joue à . . .   (for sports/see Volume 1)
Je joue de . . .   (for musical instruments, e.g. **du piano, de la guitare, de la flûte, du violon**)
Je m'intéresse à . . .   I am interested in . . .
e.g.   Je m'intéresse à la musique.

and for those things that you do **not** like doing . . .
Je déteste . . .
Je ne peux pas supporter . . .   I can't bear . . .
(this expression must be followed by a noun
e.g.   'Je ne peux pas supporter la musique pop,' dit Monsieur Gavarin.)

Here are some nouns you might want to use with 'Je ne peux pas supporter . . .'
la lecture   reading
la natation   swimming
l'aérobic   aerobics
la télévision   television
la pêche   fishing
les devoirs   homework

Une lettre
Here is a letter that Céline wrote to her friend Louise who lives in Canada.

Valréas, le dix-huit mai

Ma chère Louise,

Merci bien de ta lettre. J'ai beaucoup de travail en ce moment car je dois passer mes examens dans quelques jours. Mais hier nous avons eu un jour de congé de l'école. Le matin, j'ai aidé ma mère à faire le ménage et Marc a fait du jardinage. L'après-midi j'ai téléphoné à ma copine, Françoise, pour l'inviter à passer la soirée chez moi.

Après le souper nous avons écouté des disques et beaucoup bavardé. Nous n'avons pas regardé la télé car nous ne pouvons pas supporter les programmes que mes parents préfèrent.

Malheureusement nous n'avons pas fini nos devoirs. Je dois me lever de bonne heure demain matin pour les finir.

Comment as-tu passé le weekend dernier? As-tu joué au tennis? As-tu dansé? As-tu beaucoup travaillé?

Écris-moi vite,

Céline

New words

le travail   work
travailler   to work
passer un examen   to **take** an exam (N.B. *not*
   to pass; '**réussir à**' is one of the verbs which
   means to **pass** an exam)
un jour de congé   a day's holiday
la soirée   the evening
le souper   supper/evening meal
bavarder   to chat

Activités

1   Learn the new words.

2   Answer the following questions in English.

(a) What did Mr Gavarin do yesterday evening?
(b) What didn't he do?
(c) What did Mrs Gavarin do yesterday evening?
(d) What didn't she do?
(e) What did Céline do yesterday evening?
(f) What didn't she do?
(g) What did Marc do yesterday evening?
(h) What didn't he do?

3   Learn the negative forms of the perfect tense
given above. Then make the following sentences
negative.

(a) Madame Gavarin a voulu sortir.
(b) Marc a fait ses devoirs.
(c) Monsieur Gavarin a aidé sa femme.
(d) Céline a écrit une lettre.
(e) Nous avons pu sortir.
(f) Tu as vu tes copains?
(g) Ils ont collectionné les timbres-poste.
(h) J'ai été amateur de cinéma.
(i) Vous avez pris des photos?
(j) Elles ont collectionné les posters.

4   Learn all the new words. Then answer the
following questions in French.

(a) Tu aimes/détestes le sport?
(b) Quel sport préfères-tu?
(c) Tu joues d'un instrument musical?
(d) Quel instrument musical?
(e) Tu collectionnes les timbres-poste?
(f) Tu collectionnes les posters?
(g) Qu'est-ce que tu ne peux pas supporter?
(h) Tu aimes les animaux?
(i) Quels animaux?
(j) Tu aimes écouter des disques?

5   Ask your friend the following questions in
French.
   (Begin each question with 'Tu .....?')

(a) Do you collect records?
(b) Do you like swimming?
(c) Do you play football?
(d) Do you play the violin?
(e) Do you like watching television?
(f) Do you like making models?
(g) Do you like gardening?
(h) Do you prefer watching television?
(i) Do you like dancing?
(j) Do you do judo?

6   Learn the new words. Then write a simple
letter in French to Céline telling her what you did
last weekend in your spare time. Use the letter in
the Unit as a guide.

7   Write diary entries for last week in your
Record Book. Write in French what you did on
each day and also what you did not (forgot to) do.

e.g.   dimanche – J'ai fait mes devoirs mais je n'ai
      pas fait* mon piano.

* **faire son piano**   to do one's piano practice

   lundi – J'ai joué avec mon copain/ma copine
   mais je n'ai pas oublié de promener mon chien.

8   How would you tell someone in French
   that . . .

(a) Your brother/sister listened to records.
   (Remember to say 'mon/ma . . .' in your
   answer)
(b) He/she did not watch television.
(c) He/she collects stamps.
(d) He/she can't bear homework.
(e) He/she adores sport.

Unit 20

Au centre sportif/
At the sports centre

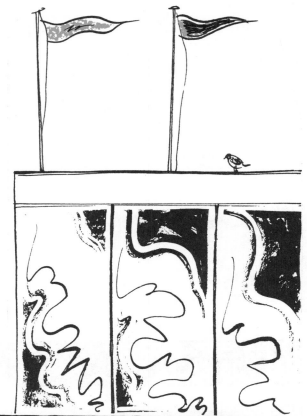

In this unit you will:
(1) *learn some useful vocabulary about sports centres;*
(2) *learn about agreement of direct objects with the perfect tense;*
(3) *revise how to give and understand directions in French.*

Le centre sportif

Au centre sportif de Valréas on peut . . .

faire de l'aérobic
faire de la gymnastique

Unit 20 continued

Dehors on peut jouer au football ou nager dans la piscine.

New words
la gymnastique   gymnastics
dehors   outside

faire du judo
jouer au badminton

jouer au basket
jouer au squash

Marc et Céline au centre sportif

Mercredi dernier Marc et Céline ont passé l'après-midi au centre sportif de Valréas. Ils y ont rencontré leurs camarades Frédéric et Françoise. Les jeunes filles ont décidé de jouer au squash à deux heures mais Céline a oublié sa nouvelle raquette. Elle l'a laissée sur la table de la cuisine. Heureusement avant de partir à deux heures et quart, Marc l'a vue sur la table et il l'a portée au centre sportif. Il l'a donnée à Céline et lui a dit 'Espèce d'idiote! Tu oublies toujours tes affaires!'

Céline l'a prise mais elle n'a pas dit 'merci'. Ses parents lui ont offert la raquette pour son anniversaire.

Les deux jeunes filles ont déjà retenu une place pour jouer au squash. Elles jouent au centre sportif chaque semaine. Mais les garçons n'ont pas retenu de place et ils ont dû donc attendre. Céline et Françoise ont commencé à jouer et les garçons les ont regardées. Mais les garçons ont bientôt commencé à les taquiner. Françoise a gagné le premier match et Frédéric lui a crié 'Bravo'. Malheureusement Marc a répété à sa soeur 'Espèce d'idiote'. Céline lui a lancé un regard plein de colère.

'J'en ai marre,' lui a-t-elle dit. 'Je vais rentrer.' Les deux amies ont quitté le centre sportif pour rentrer à la maison. Vite les deux garçons ont pris leur place et ont commencé à jouer. Ils ont joué trois matchs et Frédéric en a gagné deux.

More new words

la raquette racket
heureusement happily
espèce d'idiot(e)! Idiot!
offert offered/gave (this is the past participle of the verb 'offrir' – to offer. It is like the verb 'ouvrir'; see Unit 14 in this volume.)
déjà already
retenu (past participle of 'retenir')
chaque each
la semaine week

Unit 20 continued

donc so
taquiner to tease
gagner to win
malheureusement unfortunately
lancer un regard plein de colère to give an
  angry look
J'en ai marre I've had enough/I'm fed up

Agreement of pronoun objects

In the passage about the sports centre, you read
the following . . .

Elle l'a laiss**ée** sur la table . . .
Marc l'a vu**e**. . .
Il l'a port**ée** . . .
Il l'a donn**ée** . . .
Céline l'a pris**e** . . .

In each of the examples above an extra 'e' has
been added to the past participle. This happens
because the object of the verb is a *preceding direct
object* (l') and is feminine (it refers to 'la
raquette'). Agreements of this kind are made *only*
if the object is *direct* (see Unit 13 for *direct object
pronouns*) and if the direct object is placed in front
of the verb in the perfect tense.

You also read . . .
Les garçons les ont regard**ées** . . .

Here an extra 'es' is added to the past participle
because the *preceding direct object* ('les') refers to
Céline and Françoise (feminine plural).

Question 9 in Activité 1 could have also read
Combien de matchs . . . ont-ils jou**és**?

Here the direct object is 'Combien de matchs'. It,
too, is placed before the verb and therefore an
agreement must be made with the past participle
(gagné). An 's' is added because 'matchs' is
masculine plural.

Here are some more examples of *preceding direct
object* agreements.

(a) Tu as rencontré ma mère?
  Oui, je l'ai rencontr**ée** au supermarché.
(b) Il **m**'a rencontr**ée** en ville.
  (The 'me' refers to a woman or girl.)
(c) Il **nous** a rencontr**és** en ville.
  (The 'nous' refers to plural male or to male and
  female together.)
(d) Il **nous** a rencontr**ées** en ville.
  (The 'nous' refers to plural female)
(e) Où sont les cartes postales que j'ai achet**ées**?
  (The direct object 'les cartes postales' still
  precedes the verb in this sentence.)

New word

le rond-point roundabout

Activités

1 Learn all the new words. Then answer the
  following questions in French.
(a) Où Céline et Marc ont-ils passé l'après-midi
  mercredi dernier?
(b) Qui ont-ils rencontré là?
(c) Qu'est-ce que les jeunes filles ont décidé de
  faire?
(d) Qu'est-ce que Céline a oublié?
(e) Où l'a-t-elle laissée?
(f) Qui l'a vue?
(g) Qu'est-ce que Céline et Françoise ont fait
  d'avance?
(h) Qui a gagné le premier match?
(i) Les deux garçons ont joué combien de matchs?
(j) Qui a gagné un match seulement?

2 Answer the following questions in the
  affirmative. Say that you have left it(them) at
  home. Make any necessary agreement at the end
  of the past participle.
e.g. Tu as oublié ta raquette?
    Oui, je l'ai laiss**ée** à la maison.
(a) Tu as oublié ton maillot?
(b) Tu as oublié ta serviette?
(c) Tu as oublié tes baskets?
(d) Tu as oublié ton blouson?
(e) Tu as oublié tes chaussettes?

3 Add the correct ending to the past participle in
  the following sentences.
e.g. Combien de pommes as-tu achet**ées**?
(a) Combien de livres as-tu acheté.?
(b) Combien de matchs as-tu gagné.?
(c) Combien de boîtes as-tu acheté..?
(d) Combien d'enfants as-tu vu.?
(e) Combien de cartes postales as-tu acheté..?

4 Add the correct ending to the past participles
  in the following sentences *where necessary*.
(a) Où est la raquette que j'ai acheté?
(b) Où sont les chaussures que j'ai acheté?
(c) Où est le journal que j'ai acheté?
(d) Il nous a vu en ville. (*referring to Marc and
  Céline*)
(e) Elle m'a vu en ville. (*referring to Marc*)
(f) J'ai gagné deux matchs.
(g) J'ai laissé ma raquette à la maison.
(h) Je l'ai laissé à la maison (*referring to 'la
  raquette'*)
(i) J'ai vu mes amies.
(j) Je les ai vu. (*referring to 'les amies'*)

5 You are looking for the sports centre in a French town. How would you ask in French . . .

(a) How do I get to the Tourist Information Office, please?

(b) How do I get to the sports centre, please?

(c) Is it far?

(d) Is there a sports' centre near here, please?

(e) Do I have to catch the bus? (Remember to use 'il faut prendre . . .)

6 In answer to the above questions, you hear the words given below. Explain to your family in English what you have to do.

(a) Allez tout droit puis tournez à gauche après la boulangerie.

(b) Il faut prendre l'autobus devant l'Office de Tourisme. La ligne trois.

(c) Oui, à deux kilomètres d'ici.

(d) Oui, à une centaine* de mètres.

(e) Non, vous pouvez y aller à pied.

* **une centaine de**   about 100

7 Give the following directions in French.

e.g.   Allez jusqu'au rond-point puis tournez à gauche.

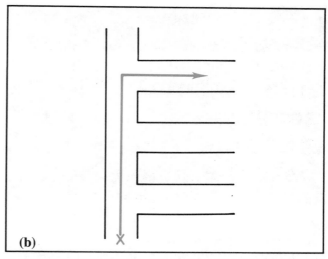
(b)

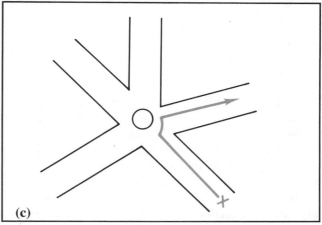
(c)

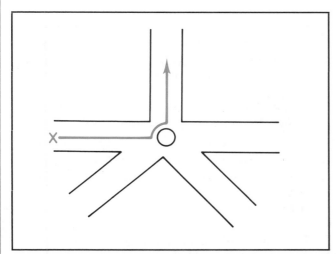
(a)

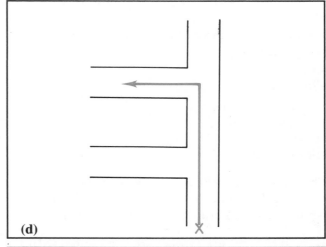
(d)

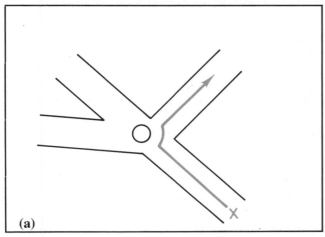
(a)

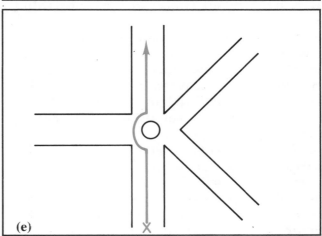
(e)

Unit 21

A la station-service/ At the petrol-station

In this unit you will learn:
(1) more about the perfect tense (with 'être');
(2) how to buy petrol and ask for other services at a garage;
(3) some important parts of the car in French.

The perfect tense: using 'être'

In Unit 17 you learnt how to form the perfect tense using 'avoir' as the auxiliary verb. However there are some verbs which have 'être' as the auxiliary verb. You must learn these verbs separately and, above all, remember which they are. Here is an example of one of these verbs in the perfect tense. Look carefully at the use of 'être' and especially at the agreement of the *past participle* (allé) with the *subject* of the verb.

aller   to go
je **suis** allé (e)   I went/have gone,

tu **es** allé(e)   etc.
il **est** allé
elle **est** allée

nous **sommes** allé(e)s
vous **êtes** allé(e)(s)
ils **sont** allés
elles **sont** allées

The letters in brackets above are used if the subject is feminine ('e') or plural ('s'). The letters which are not in brackets are always used.

Here are more verbs which are conjugated with 'être' in the perfect tense.

arriver	je **suis** arrivé(e)	I arrived
entrer	je **suis** entré(e)	I entered
monter	je **suis** monté(e)	I went up
rentrer	je **suis** rentré(e)	I went back
rester	je **suis** resté(e)	I stayed
retourner	je **suis** retourné(e)	I returned
tomber	je **suis** tombé(e)	I fell
partir	je **suis** parti(e)	I left
sortir	je **suis** sorti(e)	I went out
descendre	je **suis** descendu(e)	I went down
devenir	je **suis** devenu(e)	I became
revenir	je **suis** revenu(e)	I came back
venir	je **suis** venu(e)	I came

A la station-service

Dimanche dernier la famille Gavarin est partie de bonne heure de Valréas. Ils sont partis en voiture passer la journée à la campagne. D'abord ils sont allés à la station-service pour faire le plein d'essence. Quand ils y sont arrivés, Monsieur Gavarin est descendu de la voîture. Il a parlé à l'employé au kiosque.

Monsieur Gavarin: C'est libre-service, monsieur?
Employé: Non, monsieur. Il faut attendre le pompiste. Je vais en appeler un. Pierre, la pompe deux, s'il vous plaît.
Pompiste (à Monsieur Gavarin): Oui, monsieur?
Monsieur Gavarin: Vingt litres de super s'il vous plaît. Voulez-vous vérifier le niveau d'huile aussi?
Pompiste: Voilà, monsieur. Ça fait cent sept francs. Vous n'avez pas besoin d'huile.

Monsieur Gavarin a payé le pompiste puis il est monté dans la voiture. La famille a continué son chemin. Mais dix minutes plus tard 'Pan!' la voiture est tombée en panne.

'Mais qu'est-ce qui est arrivé?' a crié Madame Gavarin.

Toute la famille est descendue de la voiture. Madame Gavarin est devenue très inquiète.

'C'est une crevaison,' a dit Monsieur Gavarin. Il est allé chercher la roue de secours dans le coffre.

'Mais elle n'est pas là, la roue de secours. J'ai dû la laisser au garage. Nous devons retourner à la station-service à pied chercher un mécanicien.'

Monsieur Gavarin et Marc sont retournés à la station-service et Madame Gavarin et Céline sont restées dans la voiture. Une heure plus tard Monsieur Gavarin et Marc sont revenus avec le mécanicien et une roue de secours. Monsieur Gavarin a aidé le mécanicien à changer la roue mais après, il s'est senti si fatigué que la famille a décidé de rentrer à la maison!

New words

de bonne heure   early
faire le plein d'essence   to fill up with petrol
le kiosque   kiosk
libre-service   self-service
le pompiste   the petrol-pump attendant
la pompe   pump
'super'   4-star petrol
vérifier   to check
le niveau   level
l'huile (f)   oil
continuer son chemin   to go on one's way
'Pan'   'Bang'
tomber en panne   to break down
arriver   (also) to happen
inquiet/inquiète   anxious
une crevaison   puncture
la roue de secours   the spare wheel
le coffre   boot (of a car)
le mécanicien   mechanic
se sentir   to feel

The parts of a car

Here is a picture of a car. Learn all the parts of the car carefully.

bonnet   **le capot**
boot   **le coffre**
brakes   **les freins**
bumper   **le pare-chocs**
clutch   **l'embrayage** (m)
door   **la portière**
driving-mirror   **le rétroviseur**
engine   **le moteur**
headlamp   **le phare**
horn   **l'avertisseur**
indicator light   **le feu clignotant**
petrol-tank   **le réservoir à essence**
radiator   **le radiateur**
safety-belt   **la ceinture de sécurité**
seat   **le siège**
side-light   **le feu de position**
steering-wheel   **le volant**
tyre   **le pneu**
window   **la glace**
windscreen   **le pare-brise**
windscreen wiper   **l'essuie-glace** (m)

Activités

1 Learn the list of verbs which are conjugated with 'être' in the perfect tense. Learn how the perfect tense of these verbs is formed with 'être'.

2 Complete the following sentences with the correct part of the perfect tense. Pay special attention to the agreement of the past participle with the subject of the verb.

(a) Monsieur Gavarin (aller) à la station-service.
(b) Les enfants (descendre) de la voiture.
(c) Je (rester) à la maison.
(d) Vous (venir) à pied.
(e) Nous (partir) à huit heures.
(f) Madame Gavarin (sortir) de la maison.
(g) Tu (arriver) à neuf heures et demie.
(h) Elles (devenir) fatiguées.
(i) Elle (entrer) dans le magasin.
(j) Ils (retourner) à la maison.

3 Now say what the completed sentences mean in English.

4 Learn all the new words. Then answer the following questions by choosing which answer you think is the most suitable.

(a) When did the Gavarin family set out for a drive in the country?
  (i) last month
  (ii) last week
  (iii) last Saturday
  (iv) last Sunday

(b) Where did they stop first?
  (i) at a petrol-station
  (ii) at the corner shop
  (iii) at a self-service café
  (iv) at some traffic-lights

(c) Why did they stop there?
  (i) to check the tyres
  (ii) to buy some sweets at the kiosk
  (iii) to fill up with petrol
  (iv) because the children were feeling sick

(d) Where was the assistant when Monsieur Gavarin spoke to him?
  (i) in front of the petrol-pumps
  (ii) behind the petrol-pumps
  (iii) at the pay-desk
  (iv) at the car-wash

(e) What did Monsieur Gavarin want to know?
  (i) if it was a self-service garage
  (ii) if there were any free gifts
  (iii) what time it was
  (iv) how long he would have to wait

(f) What did Monsieur Gavarin ask the pump-attendant?
  (i) for petrol and the free gift
  (ii) for petrol and a windscreen-wash
  (iii) for petrol and an oil check
  (iv) for quick service

(g) What did the pump-attendant tell Monsieur Gavarin?
  (i) He had a flat tyre.
  (ii) He would not accept a credit card.
  (iii) He needed oil.
  (iv) He didn't need oil.

(h) Who went to the garage with Monsieur Gavarin after the puncture?
  (i) Madame Gavarin
  (ii) Marc
  (iii) Céline
  (iv) the mechanic

(i) Who stayed in the car?
  (i) Madame Gavarin on her own
  (ii) Madame Gavarin and the children
  (iii) Madame Gavarin and Marc
  (iv) Madame Gavarin and Céline

(j) What did the Gavarin family do when the spare wheel was changed?
  (i) They continued their journey.
  (ii) They went back home.
  (iii) They took the mechanic back to the garage.
  (iv) They had a rest.

5 You are at a service-station in France. How would you ask the following in French? Use the passage to help you.

(a) Is it self-service?
(b) Will you fill up with petrol, please?
(c) Will you check the oil level, please?
(d) Will you check the water level, please?
(e) How much is it?

6 At the service-station you hear the following. Tell your parents what the assistant says.

(a) Non, ce n'est pas libre-service.
(b) Je fais le plein d'essence?
(c) Vous avez besoin d'huile.
(d) Vous avez besoin d'eau.
(e) Ça fait cent vingt francs.

7 In your Record Book, draw a car (or stick in a cut-out car). Label all the parts in French.

Unit 22

En retard pour l'école/ Late for school

In this unit you will learn:
(1) the perfect tense of reflexive verbs;
(2) more about French schools;
(3) how to tell someone in French about your school and the subjects you study.

The perfect tense: reflexive verbs

All reflexive verbs in French are conjugated with the verb 'être'. They have the same endings as the verbs in the perfect tense which you learnt in Unit 21. Here is an example of the perfect tense of the reflexive verb 'se lever':

je me **suis** levé(e)   I got up,
tu t'**es** levé(e)   etc.
il s'**est** levé
elle s'**est** levée
nous nous **sommes** levé(e)s
vous vous **êtes** levé(e)(s)
ils se **sont** levés
elles se **sont** levées

In the following passage you will see more examples of the perfect tense of reflexive verbs.

En retard pour l'école

Dimanche soir Céline est sortie avec des amies. Les jeunes filles sont allées chez leur copine Véronique, qui les a invitées à une boum. Tout le monde s'est bien amusé. On a dansé, écouté des disques et beaucoup bavardé. Céline est rentrée tard.

D'habitude, le matin, elle se lève avant Marc. Quand le réveil sonne à sept heures, c'est toujours Céline qui se lève la première mais lundi dernier elle ne s'est pas réveillée à l'heure. Elle n'a pas entendu le réveil. Marc n'a pas de réveil dans sa chambre car c'est toujours sa soeur qui le réveille le matin. Alors lundi dernier il ne s'est pas réveillé à l'heure non plus.

Ce matin-là Madame Gavarin est sortie de bonne heure avec Monsieur Gavarin. Elle est allée à la gare routière. Souvent le lundi, elle va voir une vieille tante qui habite à Avignon. La tante Jeanne a quatre-vingt-sept ans. Elle souffre de ses jambes et elle marche avec difficulté.

Lundi dernier Marc s'est réveille à huit heures et demie. Il a regardé sa montre puis s'est levé d'un bond.

'Huit heures et demie! Mais les cours ont déjà commencé. Où est Céline?' a dit Marc.

Il a appelé sa soeur. 'Mon Dieu!' s'est écriée Céline. 'Nous devons nous dépêcher.'

Les deux enfants se sont vite lavés puis ils se sont habillés. Ils n'ont pas pris le petit déjeuner ce jour-là. Ils ont quitté la maison à neuf heures moins dix. Ils ont couru le long de la rue jusqu'à l'arrêt d'autobus. Un autobus est bientôt arrivé mais les enfants sont arrivés en retard pour leur deuxième cours.

Unit 22 *continued*

New words

une boum   a party
s'amuser   to enjoy oneself
le réveil   alarm-clock
entendre   to hear
non plus   neither
souffrir   to suffer (conjugates like 'ouvrir')
un bond   leap
un cours   lesson
Mon Dieu!   Goodness me!
s'écrier   to exclaim
ce jour-là   that particular day
courir   to run
le long de   along

L'emploi du temps

Here is Marc's timetable

	lundi	*mardi*	*mercredi*
8–9h	maths	anglais	histoire
9–10h	anglais	sciences naturelles	maths
10–11h	travaux manuels	géographie	français
11–12h	travaux manuels	français	géographie
L'heure du déjeuner			
2–3h	français	maths	—
3–4h	chimie	physique	—
4–5h	chimie	physique	—

	jeudi	*vendredi*	*samedi*
8–9h	français	travaux pratiques	maths
9–10h	histoire	gymnastique	anglais
10–11h	dessin	français	français
11–12h	dessin	instruction civique	—
L'heure du déjeuner			
2–3h	maths	anglais	
3–4h	travaux pratiques	maths	
4–5	musique	perme	

These are the subjects that Marc studies. How many are the same as the subjects you study?

l'anglais   English
la chimie   Chemistry
le dessin   Art
le français   French
la géographie   Geography
la gymnastique   Gymnastics
l'histoire (*f*)   History
l'instruction civique (*f*)   Civics
les maths   Maths
la musique   Music
la physique   Physics
les sciences naturelles   Natural science
les travaux manuels   ⎱ craft
les travaux pratiques ⎰
'perme' (une heure de perme)   a free lesson (supervised)

Here are some more subjects which you perhaps study.
l'allemand   German
l'espagnol   Spanish
le latin   Latin
l'instruction religieuse   RE
les sports   Games

French schools

As you can see from Marc's timetable the French school day is longer than yours and each lesson is longer too. Marc has to go to school on Saturday morning. He goes to a state school, but many private schools (**école libre**) have lessons on Monday to Friday as you do. Children who live in rural areas in France often go to these private schools (they are not as expensive as in this country) and are boarders during the week but return home for the weekend. In French schools, pupils who have 'une heure de perme (permanence)' at the end of morning or afternoon school are allowed to go home. There is no Assembly in French schools nor Registration. Each subject teacher keeps an attendance record for each class. There is no corporal punishment but matters of discipline are the concern of the **censeur** (Pastoral Deputy Head) who can impose **une heure de 'colle'** (detention – supervised by **un surveillant**). Pupils who do not reach the required standard at the end of the academic year have to stay in the same class for a further year (**redoubler**).

Activités

1 Read the passage carefully and then learn all the new words.

2 Answer the following questions by choosing the most suitable of the answers given.

(a) Where did Céline go last Sunday evening?
  (i) to the cinema
  (ii) to a party
  (iii) out with a friend
  (iv) to visit her aunt

(b) When did she return home?
  (i) late
  (ii) early
  (iii) the next morning
  (iv) the next afternoon

(c) When does Céline normally get up?
  (i) at 6.30
  (ii) at 7.30
  (iii) before Marc
  (iv) after Marc

(d) What happened last Monday?
  (i) She woke up early.
  (ii) She woke up when Madame Gavarin called her.
  (iii) She woke up when Monsieur Gavarin called her.
  (iv) She woke up when Marc called her.

(e) Why didn't Marc hear the alarm?
  (i) He was so tired.
  (ii) He forgot to set the alarm.
  (iii) The alarm had stopped.
  (iv) He doesn't have an alarm.

(f) Where was Madame Gavarin?
  (i) in the kitchen
  (ii) in the garden
  (iii) she had gone visiting
  (iv) she had gone shopping

(g) How old is Aunt Jeanne?
  (i) 87
  (ii) 86
  (iii) 96
  (iv) 97

(h) What is wrong with her?
  (i) She has a broken leg.
  (ii) She has trouble with her legs.
  (iii) She has sprained her ankle.
  (iv) She is paralysed.

(i) What didn't Marc and Céline do before going to school?
  (i) wash
  (ii) dress properly
  (iii) have breakfast
  (iv) make their beds

(j) At what time did they leave the house?
  (i) 9.10
  (ii) 9.20
  (iii) 8.40
  (iv) 8.50

3 Learn all the new words. The names of subjects (**les matières**) in French begin with a small letter.

4 In your Record Book write out your timetable. Give the day, time and subject in French. French school children do not have **la recréation** ('Break') as you do in secondary schools.

5 Answer the following questions in French.

N.B. **être fort(e) en**   to be good at . . .
     être faible en   to be bad at . . .

(a) Tu aimes l'école?
(b) Tu es en quelle classe?
(c) Tu aimes les maths?
(d) Tu aimes le français?
(e) Tu es fort(e) en maths?
(f) Tu es faible en anglais?
(g) Quelle est ta matière préférée?   (favourite)
(h) Combien d'élèves y a-t-il dans ta classe de français?
(i) Comment s'appelle ton professeur de français?
(j) Tu aimes la gymnastique?

6 How would you ask a French friend of your own age the following questions?

(a) Do you like school?
(b) What class are you in?
(c) Do you like English?
(d) Are you good at English?
(e) Do you like Physics?
(f) What is your favourite subject?
(g) How many teachers are there in your school?
(h) Do you like Games?
(i) Do you go to school on Saturday morning?
  (**le samedi matin**)
  N.B. 'on' is not translated
(j) Do you go to school on Wednesday afternoon?

Unit 23

La maison de la presse/ The newsagent's

In this unit you will:
(1) learn how to use stressed pronouns;
(2) learn something of the French press;
(3) look at an advertising extract from a French newspaper.

La maison de la presse se trouve dans la rue principale de Valréas. Un touriste anglais veut acheter un journal anglais. Il a stationné sa voiture sur la Place de la Poste mais il ne sait pas où aller. Devant lui se trouve le bureau de poste et derrière lui il y a un café. Il décide d'y aller prendre un verre avant de chercher la maison de la presse.

Une demi-heure plus tard, il demande au garçon de café 'Pour aller à la maison de la presse, s'il vous plaît?'

'Prenez cette rue en face de vous. Allez jusqu'au rond-point, puis tournez à droite. La maison de la presse se trouve en face de l'église,' dit le garçon.

Le touriste répète, 'Cette rue en face de moi? Jusqu'au rond-point? Puis à droite et la maison de la presse se trouve en face de moi?'

'Non, monsieur, en face de l'église,' répond le garçon.

'Mais oui, en face de l'église. Je me suis trompé,' dit le touriste.

New words

principal(e) main
le journal newspaper
prendre un verre to have a drink (of wine)
une demi-heure half an hour
se tromper to make a mistake

Stressed pronouns

These are . . .

moi me
toi you
lui him
elle her
nous us
vous you
eux them (*masculine*)
elles them (*feminine*)

In this Unit you have seen some of these stressed pronouns used with *prepositions*
e.g. **devant lui** in front of him
derrière lui behind him
en face de moi in front of me
en face de vous in front of you

and you have already seen some of them in earlier units. Learn all the new ones carefully. Here are some more prepositions which you have already learnt, and which are often used with stressed pronouns:

chez at . . . house
à côté de by the side of/beside
près de near to
pour for

As you learn more French you will learn of other occasions where stressed (*disjunctive*) pronouns are used.

La maison de la presse

A la maison de la presse on peut acheter les quotidiens, les magazines, les revues et aussi la papeterie et les livres. Dans les grandes villes on voit souvent des kiosques à journaux, où on vend les cartes et les cartes postales aussi. En été on trouve souvent des journaux étrangers dans les grandes villes françaises. Les journaux les mieux connus en France sont *Le Figaro* et *Le Monde*.

Chaque région a son propre journal aussi, e.g. *Le Progrès* de Lyon. *Paris Match* est un des magazines les plus populaires pour les adultes. Pour les jeunes (les adolescents) il y a beaucoup de magazines sur la musique pop, e.g. *Salut* et *Hit Magazine*. Pour les plus jeunes il y a des magazines de bandes dessinées. Pour eux *Tintin*, *Lucky Luke* et *Astérix* sont les personnages favoris.

New words

le quotidien   daily paper
la revue   magazine
la papeterie   stationery
les journaux   newspapers (plural of **journal**)
étranger   foreign
les mieux connus   the best known
propre   own
populaire   popular
les adultes   adults
au sujet de   about
la musique pop   pop music
la bande dessinée   cartoon
le personnage   character

Unit 23 continued

Here is an extract from a French newspaper advertising *Magicville* in the south of France. You will be surprised how much of the paper you can understand. With the knowledge of some key words you will be able to tell your parents and friends what there is to offer there.

Look carefully at the main headline:

'En famille, petits et grands, papas, mamans, venez rire, venez faire la fête!'

New words

rire   to laugh
faire la fête   to have a good time/to celebrate

Key words in the adverts

Trétaux aux 4 vents   Travelling theatre
la kermesse   fair
le dessin animé   cartoon
Guignol, Gnafron, Polichinelle   puppets
l'auberge   inn

Activités

1. Learn the new words. Then answer the following questions in French.

(a) Où se trouve la maison de la presse?

(b) Qu'est-ce que le touriste anglais veut acheter?

(c) Où a-t-il stationné sa voiture?

(d) Le touriste sait où se trouve la maison de la presse?

(e) Qu'est-ce qu'il y a devant lui?

(f) Qu'est-ce qu'il y a derrière lui?

(g) Où est-il allé d'abord?

(h) Combien de temps* est-il resté au café?

(i) La maison de la presse se trouve derrière l'église?

(j) Qui s'est trompé?

* **Combien de temps** How long?

2. Give the French for . . .

(a) For me

(b) For them (*masculine*)

(c) In front of us

(d) In front of you (*speaking to a stranger*)

(e) Beside him

(f) Opposite you (*speaking to a stranger*)

(g) Near to me

(h) For them (*feminine*)

(i) Behind you (*to a friend*)

(j) At her house.

3. Learn all the new words. Then answer the following questions in French.

(a) Qu'est-ce qu'on peut acheter à la maison de la presse?

(b) Où voit-on souvent des kiosques à journaux?

(c) Qu'est-ce qu'on y vend aussi?

(d) Qu'est-ce qu'on peut y trouver en été?

(e) Quels sont les journaux les mieux connus en France?

(f) Comment s'appelle le journal de la région de Lyon?

(g) Quel est un des magazines les plus populaires en France?

(h) Quels sont les magazines pour les jeunes au sujet de la musique pop?

(i) Qu'est-ce qu'il y a pour les plus jeunes?

(j) Tu aimes les bandes dessinées?

4. You are at a newsagent's or a newspaper-stand in France. How would you ask for the following? (Remember to use the polite 'vous' form of the verb where necessary.)

(a) Do you have any English newspapers?

(b) How much is it?

(c) Do you have a map of the region?

(d) Do you have any postcards?

(e) What magazines do you have for young people (**les jeunes**)?

5. Look carefully at the newspaper and then answer the following questions in English.

(a) At what time does the super show begin in the Village Gaulois?

(b) How many hours of aerobics and dance are there each day?

(c) How many shows are there each day at the Music Hall?

(d) What age range can try the 'cyclo-kart'?

(e) How long is the 'Jardin de Magicville' open each day?

Unit 24

Le bureau des objets trouvés/ The lost property office

In this unit you will:
(1) *learn more about formal letter writing;*
(2) *practise asking about lost property;*
(3) *revise expressions of need and obligation;*
(4) *learn expressions of pleasure/displeasure.*

Formal letter writing

In Unit 11 you saw an example of a formal letter written to the Syndicat D'Initiative at Rennes. When writing a formal letter, the word for 'Dear' is not used at the beginning. The letter should begin with . . .

Monsieur,
(or) **Madame,**
(or) **Mademoiselle.**

There is also a very polite formal ending to the letter . . .

Je vous prie d'agréer Monsieur (Madame, Mademoiselle) l'expression de mes sentiments distingués.

There are certain other polite expressions which are used in formal letters. You will learn some later in this Unit.

Your address should be given in the top left-hand corner. The recipient's address should be given on the right-hand side under the town and the date. Check back to Unit 11 to see the layout of a formal letter.

Here is another example of a formal letter. You have been on holiday in France where you lost your camera (**un appareil**). You have already written to the 'Bureau des objets trouvés' and here is their answer . . .

Paris, le 2 septembre

Mademoiselle,

     J'accuse réception de votre lettre du 25 août. Nous ferons tout notre possible pour vous aider. D'abord nous devons vous poser quelques questions. Pouvez-vous préciser la date où vous avez perdu votre appareil et si c'est possible le lieu exact? Si vous ne savez pas exactement où vous l'avez perdu, pouvez-vous nous indiquer le quartier de la ville où vous pensez l'avoir perdu? Et quelle est la marque de l'appareil?

     En attendant de vous lire, veuillez agréer, Mademoiselle, l'expression de mes sentiments distingués.

Philippe Leclerc
Philippe Leclerc

New words

J'accuse réception de . . .
I acknowledge receipt of . . .
Nous ferons tout notre possible . . .
We will do everything possible . . .
poser to put
préciser to specify
le lieu place/spot
exactement exactly
le quartier district
penser to think
la marque make/brand name
En attendant vous lire while waiting to hear
from you
**veuillez agréer l'expression de mes
sentiments distingués** (this is another way of
saying . . 'Yours faithfully')

Dans la rue

You have failed to find the 'Bureau des objets
trouvés'. You need to ask for directions.

Vous: Pardon, monsieur, je dois trouver le bureau
des objets trouvés. J'ai cherché partout* mais
je ne le vois pas. Savez-vous où il se trouve, s'il
vous plaît?
Passant: Il faut descendre cette rue, puis tournez
à droite aux feux. Le bureau des objets trouvés
est à côté du Syndicat d'Initiative.
Vous: Merci, monsieur.
Passant: De rien, mademoiselle.
* **partout** everywhere

A letter to the campsite

Last year the Gavarins' cousins – the Latille
family – spent a holiday at a campsite in France.
Madame Latille left her ring in the washrooms.
Monsieur Latille has written a letter to the
warden asking about the ring and at the same
time tells him what they liked and disliked about
the campsite.

Rémuzat, le 4 septembre

Monsieur,

En rentrant chez nous après deux
semaines de vacances, ma femme m'a dit qu'elle
a laissé sa bague d'or dans le bloc sanitaire de
votre camping. Nous avons quitté le camping le
30 août et m'a femme a perdu sa bague ce
matin-là. Si vous l'avez trouvée, je vous serai
reconnaissant de bien vouloir me l'envoyer.

Nous sommes restés dix jours au camping et
nous l'avons trouvé propre et bien entretenu.
Malheureusement le choix au libre-service est
très limité et nous avons dû aller en ville
acheter nos provisions.

Nos enfants ont bien apprécié les aires de
jeux mais ma femme pense qu'elles sont trop
près des poubelles. Néanmoins tout le monde
s'est bien amusé et nous avons l'intention d'y
retourner l'année prochaine.

En attendant votre réponse, je vous prie
d'agréer, Monsieur, l'expression de mes
sentiments distingués.

M. Latille

New words

en rentrant on returning
la bague d'or gold ring
**je vous serai reconnaissant de bien
vouloir** . . .
I shall be grateful if you will . . .
propre clean
bien entretenu well-kept
le choix choice
le libre-service self-service shop
limité limited
apprécier to appreciate
les aires de jeux the play areas
néanmoins however
la réponse reply

Idiomatic expressions

The Latille children enjoyed their holiday very
much. Here are some of the words they use to
describe their holiday . . .

Superbe!
Sensas! } Great!
Génial!
Chouette!

When they don't like something they often say . . .

C'est casse-pieds! It's a pain!
C'est ennuyeux! It's boring!

Activités

1 Learn the new words. Then answer the questions in English

(a) Is Philippe Leclerc going to help you?
(b) Does he say if the camera has been found?
(c) What information does he require?
(d) Using the same formal beginning and ending as given in the letter opposite, write (in your Record Book) a letter in French to Philippe Leclerc giving the details he requires. Tell him that you lost your camera on 15 August in (**sur**) the Place de la Concorde. Tell him that your camera is a Kodak.

2 If you lose something in France you may report the loss to the police. You are at the police-station (**le commissariat de police**) in France to report a loss. Here are the policeman's questions. Answer them in French.

(a) Vous avez perdu quelque chose?
(Say yes and that you have lost a camera.)
(b) Savez-vous exactement où vous l'avez perdu?
(Say that you lost it near the church.)
(c) Quand l'avez-vous perdu?
(Say that you lost it this morning.)
(d) Quelle est la marque de l'appareil?
(Say that it is an Agfa.)
(e) Nous n'avons pas d'appareils trouvés de la marque Agfa. Je vous conseille d'aller demander au bureau des objets trouvés qui se trouve à côté du Syndicat d'Initiative.
(Thank the policeman and say goodbye.)

3 Explain in English how to get to the Bureau Des Objets Trouvés according to the passer-by in the conversation 'Dans la rue'.

4 Je dois . . .
You are in France and need to find the following places. Tell your French friend . . .

e.g. I must go to the lost property office.
 Je dois aller au bureau des objets trouvés.

(a) I must go to the bank.
(b) I must go to the post office.
(c) We must go to the chemist's.
(d) We must go to the railway station.
(e) I must go to the tourist information office.

5 Il faut . . .
You are giving your French friend directions. Use 'Il faut . . .' in your answers. Tell him/her . . .

e.g. You must go to the lost property office.
 Il faut aller au bureau des objets trouvés.

(a) You must go down this street.
(b) You must turn left at the traffic lights.
(c) You must cross the bridge.
(d) You must catch the bus.
(e) You must go as far as the roundabout.

6 Au 'Bureau des objets trouvés'
You have now found the Lost Property Office.

(a) Say good morning to the assistant (a man).
(b) Say that you have lost your watch (**la montre**).
(c) Say that you lost it yesterday.
(d) Say that you lost it in the park.
(e) Say that it is a digital* watch.

* **digital(e)** digital (place after the noun)

7 Learn the new words and expressions. Then answer the following questions in English.

(a) How long were the Latilles away on holiday?
(b) Where did Madame Latille leave her ring?
(c) When did the family leave the campsite?
(d) How long had they stayed there?
(e) What did they like about the campsite?
(f) What did the children particularly like?
(g) What did they think of the shop on the campsite?
(h) Why did they go into town?
(i) What did Madame Latille think about the play areas?
(j) What do the family intend to do next year?

8 In your Record Book re-write the letter given above with the following changes . . .

(a) you were on holiday for four weeks
(b) your mother left her watch in the washrooms
(c) you left the campsite on 2 September
(d) you stayed for three weeks at the campsite
(e) you did *not* find the site clean
(f) there is a good (**grand**) choice of goods at the self-service shop
(g) you did not have to go to town for your goods
(h) you liked the swimming-pool but it was too near the restaurant
(i) however, everyone enjoyed themselves
(j) you intend to return there next year.

9 Which word(s) would you use to describe the following to your French friend . . .

(a) le collège
(b) le week-end
(c) le lundi
(d) le français
(e) les vacances

Unit 25

A la banque/Au bureau de change – At the bank/ At the foreign exchange office

In this unit you will:
(1) revise numbers and currency in French;
(2) practise changing money and travellers' cheques at a bank or foreign exchange office;
(3) play a numbers game.

Voici un chèque de voyage

On peut toucher un chèque de voyage et changer des billets de banque en France dans les banques et dans les bureaux de change. Mais vous devez aussi présenter votre passeport en même temps. Écoutez cette conversation à la banque entre une touriste et l'employé.

Touriste: Bonjour, monsieur, je voudrais toucher un chèque de voyage. Où faut-il aller?

Employé: Au guichet là-bas, mademoiselle.

Touriste: Quel guichet, monsieur, s'il vous plaît?

Employé: Au guichet marqué 'Change', mademoiselle.

Touriste: Merci, monsieur.

(cinq minutes plus tard, au guichet marqué 'Change')

Touriste: Je voudrais toucher un chèque de voyage, mademoiselle. Combien vaut la livre sterling aujourd'hui, s'il vous plaît?

Employée: Onze francs trente. Vous avez votre passeport, mademoiselle?

Touriste: Oh, je l'ai laissé à l'hôtel. Je dois aller le chercher.

New words

toucher un chèque de voyage   to cash a travellers' cheque

en même temps   at the same time

combien vaut . .?   how much is . . . worth?

la livre sterling   English pound

Other words

Here are some more words that you might hear at the bank/exchange office.

Il faut signer ici   You must sign here

Il faut présenter la fiche à la caisse
You must take the form to the cash-desk.

If you wish to change English bank notes into francs you should say . . .

Je voudrais changer des livres sterling en francs.

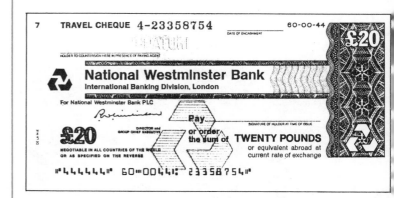

Activités

1 Learn all the new words and expressions.

2 You are at a bank/exchange office in France. Give the following information in French.

(a) Say good-morning to the assistant (female) and say you would like to cash a travellers' cheque.

(b) Ask which counter, please.

(c) Ask how much the pound is worth today.

(d) Say that you have your passport.

(e) Ask if you have to sign.

(f) Ask where the cash-desk is.

(g) Thank the assistant and say goodbye.

3 Here are some answers that you might hear. Tell your parents what the assistant is saying.

(a) Allez au guichet là-bas, à gauche.

(b) Onze francs quarante.

(c) Il faut signer là.

(d) La caisse est à droite.

(e) Vous avez votre passeport?

4 You have the following amounts of English currency to change. Work out how many francs you should receive if the exchange rate is £1 to 11f 30. (In reality you would have an amount deducted as a service charge. This amount varies according to where you change your money. In this Activité you may ignore the service charge.)

(a) £10
(b) £5
(c) £20
(d) £25
(e) £15

5 Here is a 'fiche' which was used to change travellers' cheques in the *Banque Nationale de Paris*. Look at it carefully then answer the following questions in English.

Here are some of the key words to help you:

codes des devises Currency codes
codes des transactions Transaction codes

achat TC buying (by the bank from the customer) travellers' cheques.

montant en devise the amount of (foreign) currency

cours Exchange rate

montant en FRF amount in francs

commission service charge

(a) On what date was the transaction made?

(b) How much was changed and from what currency?

(c) What was the exchange rate in francs?

(d) What was the service charge? Give the amount in
  (i) francs
and (ii) sterling.

(e) How much did the tourist actually receive? Give the amount in (i) francs
  and (ii) sterling.

BANQUE NATIONALE DE PARIS
SOCIÉTÉ ANONYME AU CAPITAL DE 1.632.580.000 FRANCS
SIÈGE SOCIAL: 16, BOULEVARD DES ITALIENS PARIS 9ª
R.C.S. PARIS B 662 042 449

BORDEREAU de CHANGE

Code Guichet	00799
Date	25 4 1934
Nº du Bordereau	33
Code devise	6
Code transaction	3
Montant en devise	100·00
Cours	11·5033
Montant en FRF	1,150·33
Commission	7·50
Espèces	1,143·03
Compte	- · - - - · · ·

CODES DES DEVISES

1 Deutsche Mark - Allemagne
2 Franc Belge
3 Dollar - Canada
4 Peseta - Espagne
5 Dollar - USA
6 Livre Sterling - GB
7 Lire - Italie
8 Florin - Pays Bas
9 Escudo - Portugal
10 Franc Suisse
11 Diverses

CODES DES TRANSACTIONS

1 Achat BB
2 Vente BB
3 Achat TC

Nom
Prénom
Adresse

Nº Passeport:

FG.1166 10-82

6 Now give all your answers to Activité 5 in French. If you need to revise the numbers in French, check back to Volume I, and also Unit 7 in this Volume.

A numbers game – à la banque

The following game may be played by any number of players. Each player should have a coloured counter to place on the numbers.

To begin the game each player must throw six on the dice. When he/she has thrown six, he/she may throw the dice again and then proceed to the number thrown. All counting must be in French. The first player to reach 100 is the winner, but he/she must throw the exact number to finish.

Along the way to the bank some obstacles may be encountered but also some unexpected help!

Dimanche. Recommencez. Banque fermée
Sunday. Begin again. Bank closed

L'heure du déjeuner. Manquez un tour.
Lunch-time. Miss a turn.

Vous avez perdu votre portefeuille. Recommencez.
You have lost your wallet. Begin again.

Vous avez trouvé votre portefeuille. Allez au 50.
You have found your wallet. Go to 50.

Samedi. Recommencez. Banque fermée.
Saturday. Begin again. Bank closed.

Jour férié. Manquez un tour
Bank holiday. Miss a turn.

Un coup de veine. Allez au 80(95).
A windfall/stroke of luck. Go to 80(95).

On vous a volé. Recommencez.
You have been robbed. Begin again.

LA BANQUE 100	99	ON VOUS A VOLÉ 98 RECOMMENCEZ	97	96	95	94	93	92	91
UN COUP DE VEINE 81 ALLEZ AU 95	82	83	DIMANCHE RECOMMENCEZ 84 BANQUE FERMÉE	85	86	87	88	L'HEURE DU DÉJEUNER 89 MANQUEZ UN TOUR	90
80	79	78	77	76	75	JOUR FÉRIÉ 74 MANQUEZ UN TOUR	73	72	71
61	SAMEDI RECOMMENCEZ 62 BANQUE FERMÉE	63	64	65	66	67	68	69	UN COUP DE VEINE 70 ALLEZ AU 80
60	59	58	57	L'HEURE DU DÉJEUNER 56 MANQUEZ UN TOUR	55	54	53	52	51
41	42	JOUR FÉRIÉ 43 MANQUEZ UN TOUR	44	45	46	47	DIMANCHE RECOMMENCEZ 48 BANQUE FERMÉE	49	50
SAMEDI RECOMMENCEZ 40 BANQUE FERMÉE	39	38	37	36	35	34	33	32	31
21	22	23	24	25	VOUS AVEZ PERDU VOTRE PORTEFEUILLE 26 RECOMMENCEZ	27	28	VOUS AVEZ TROUVÉ VOTRE PORTEFEUILLE 29 ALLEZ AU 50	30
20	19	18	DIMANCHE RECOMMENCEZ 17 BANQUE FERMÉE	16	15	14	13	12	L'HEURE DU DÉJEUNER 11 MANQUEZ UN TOUR
1	2	3	4	5	6	7	8	9	10

A LA BANQUE ➤➤➤

Answers

Unit 1

2 **(a)** (i)
(b) (iii)
(c) (ii)
(d) (iv)
(e) (i)
(f) (iv)
(g) (i)
(h) (iii)
(i) (ii)
(j) (ii)

3 **(a)** Elle fait des achats.
(b) Nous sommes à Londres.
(c) Tu as un bon accent.
(d) Ils vont au Syndicat d'Initiative.
(e) Je vais visiter les monuments historiques.
(f) Vous faites une promenade.
(g) Elles ont l'intention d'aller aux magasins.
(h) Je suis en vacances.
(i) Il fait beau.
(j) Vous êtes devant l'hôtel.

5 **(a)** Nous devons faire des achats.
(b) Je dois chercher un hôtel.
(c) Vous devez aller au Syndicat d'Initiative.
(d) Tu dois visiter les monuments historiques.
(e) Elles doivent acheter des robes d'hiver.
(f) Il doit aller au musée.
(g) Nous devons regarder le plan de la ville.
(h) Ils doivent voyager à Londres.
(i) Je dois partir de bonne heure.
(j) Elle doit chercher un hôtel.

6 **(a)** We must do some shopping.
(b) I must look for a hotel.
(c) You must go to the Tourist Information Office.
(d) You must visit the historic monuments.
(e) They must buy some winter dresses.
(f) He must go to the museum.
(g) We must look at the plan of the town.
(h) They must travel to London.
(i) I must leave early.
(j) She must find a hotel.

8 **(a)** On cherche une villa sur la côte d'Azur.
(b) On voyage en Europe.
(c) On reste à la campagne.
(d) On va passer les vacances à l'étranger.
(e) On fait du camping.
(f) On va rester à l'hôtel.
(g) On passe les vacances au bord de la mer.
(h) On va passer les vacances chez soi.
(i) On passe les vacances chez des parents.
(j) On va louer une villa.

10 **(a)** Allez tout droit.
(b) Prenez la deuxième rue à droite. Puis allez tout droit.
(c) Tournez à droite. Puis allez tout droit.
(d) Tournez à droite. Puis prenez la première rue à gauche.

Unit 2

2 **(a)** C'est ma tente.
(b) C'est mon sac de couchage.
(c) C'est ma chaise pliante.
(d) C'est mon réchaud.
(e) C'est ma table pliante.

3 **(a)** Où sont les douches, s'il vous plaît?
(b) Où sont les toilettes, s'il vous plaît?
(c) Où est la piscine, s'il vous plaît?
(d) Où est le bureau d'acceuil, s'il vous plaît?
(e) Où sont les poubelles, s'il vous plaît?
(f) Où est la salle de jeux, s'il vous plaît?
(g) Où est le bureau de renseignements, s'il vous plaît?
(h) Où sont les caravanes, s'il vous plaît?
(i) Où est mon sac de couchage, s'il vous plaît?
(j) Où est le bloc sanitaire, s'il vous plaît?

4 **(a)** (ii)
(b) (i)
(c) (i)
(d) (iii)
(e) (ii)
(f) (i)
(g) (i)
(h) (ii)
(i) (iv)
(j) (iv)

5 **(a)** Voilà les enfants qui jouent derrière la tente.
(b) Voilà le terrain de camping qui est au bord de la rivière.
(c) Regardez ces enfants qui pêchent dans la rivière.
(d) Je préfère notre emplacement qui est ombragé.
(e) Nous allons faire une promenade au bord de la rivière qui coule près du camping.

6 **(a)** There are the children who are playing behind the tent.
(b) There is the campsite which is by the river.
(c) Look at those children who are fishing in the river.

(d) I prefer our pitch which is shaded.
(e) We are going to go for a walk by the river which flows near the campsite.

7 **(a)** C'est un terrain de camping ombragé que nous cherchons.
(b) C'est un terrain de camping herbeux que nous cherchons.
(c) C'est un terrain de camping herbeux qu'on cherche.
(d) Voilà le camping que nous cherchons.
(e) Voici la caravane qu'on cherche.

8 **(a)** It is a shady campsite that we are looking for.
(b) It is a grassy campsite that we are looking for.
(c) It is a grassy campsite that we are (one is) looking for.
(d) There is the campsite that we are looking for.
(e) Here is the caravan that we are (one is) looking for.

9 **(a)** Oui, j'aime faire du camping./Non, je n'aime pas faire du camping.
(b) Je préfère faire du camping./Je préfère rester à l'hôtel.
(c) Oui, j'ai une tente./Non, je n'ai pas de tente.
(d) Oui, j'ai une caravane./Non, je n'ai pas de caravane.
(e) Oui, j'ai un sac de couchage./Non, je n'ai pas de sac de couchage.

10 **(a)** Le camping est tranquille?
(b) Le camping est ombragé?
(c) Il y a une piscine?
(d) Il y a un restaurant?
(e) Le camping est près de la ville?

Unit 3

2 **(a)** Meals are prepared for you.
Your bed is made for you.
(b) In your room.
In the dining-room.
(c) You can be called in the mornings if you wish.
(d) Every day.
(e) They will tidy their things themselves.

3 **(a)** Tu jettes tes affaires par terre.
(b) Nous rangeons nos affaires.
(c) J'appelle la femme de ménage.
(d) Ils appellent la femme de ménage.
(e) Nous commençons le petit déjeuner.
(f) Elle envoie une carte postale à ses amis.
(g) Je répète la question.
(h) Il espère arriver ce soir.
(i) Vous espérez rester à l'hôtel?
(j) Elles commencent leurs vacances

4 **(a)** You throw your things on the floor.
(b) We tidy up our things.
(c) I call the maid.
(d) They call the maid.
(e) We begin breakfast.
(f) She sends a postcard to her friends.
(g) I repeat the question.
(h) He hopes to arrive this evening.
(i) You hope to stay in a hotel?
(j) They begin their holidays.

6 **(a)** Two
(b) Double rooms
(c) One with a bathroom and one with a shower
(d) Three nights
(e) Yes
(f) On the third floor
(g) 90 francs a night
(h) On the first floor
(i) 112 francs a night
(j) No

7 **(a)** Avez-vous une chambre à deux lits avec salle de bain, s'il vous plaît?
(b) Avez-vous une chambre à deux lits sans salle de bain, s'il vous plaît?
(c) Avez-vous une chambre à deux lits avec douche, s'il vous plaît?
(d) Avez-vous une chambre à un lit au premier étage, s'il vous plaît?
(e) Avez-vous une chambre à deux lits au premier étage, s'il vous plaît?
(f) Il y a un ascenseur?
(g) Quel est le prix de la chambre?
(h) Le petit déjeuner est compris?

8 **(a)** yes
(b) 1200 francs
about £106

Unit 4

4 **(a)** At nine o'clock
(b) Half-past nine
(c) She goes to the bathroom.
(d) Next to her bedroom
(e) Jeans and a T-shirt
(f) A pretty dress
(g) Her grandparents don't like jeans.
(h) Put on her coat
(i) His overcoat
(j) 'Hurry up! You are always late.'

5 **(a)** Je mets mon manteau.
(b) Vous mettez votre manteau?
(c) Il met son pardessus.
(d) Elle met son manteau.
(e) Elles mettent leurs chaussures.

(f) Tu mets ton chapeau?
(g) Ils mettent leurs souliers.
(h) Nous mettons nos gants.
(i) Je mets ma nouvelle robe.
(j) Il met son gilet.

6 **(a)** I put on my coat.
(b) Are you putting on your coat?
(c) He puts on his overcoat.
(d) She puts on her coat.
(e) They put on their shoes.
(f) Are you putting on your hat?
(g) They put on their shoes.
(h) We put on our gloves.
(i) I'm putting on my new dress.
(j) He puts on his waistcoat.

7 **(a)**
   (i) Elle se réveille à huit heures.
   (ii) Nous nous lavons dans la salle de bain.
   (iii) Je mets mon blue-jean.
   (iv) Ils se lèvent à sept heures.
   (v) Vous vous couchez à dix heures.
   (vi) La salle de bain se trouve à côté de ma chambre.
   (vii) Elles se dépêchent.
   (viii) Tu te couches à neuf heures et demie.
   (ix) Je m'habille dans ma chambre.
   (x) Elle se brosse les cheveux.
   (b)
   (i) She wakes up at eight o'clock.
   (ii) We get washed in the bathroom.
   (iii) I put on my jeans.
   (iv) They get up at seven o'clock.
   (v) You go to bed at ten o'clock.
   (vi) The bathroom is next to my bedroom.
   (vii) They are hurrying.
   (viii) You go to bed at half past nine.
   (ix) I get dressed in my bedroom.
   (x) She brushes her hair.

8 **(a)** Je me réveille le dimanche à . . .
(b) Je me réveille le lundi à . . .
(c) Je m'habille dans . . .
(d) Je me lave dans . . .
(e) Le dimanche je mets . . .
(f) Le samedi je mets . . .
(g) Quand il fait froid je mets un manteau (pardessus).
(h) Quand il fait chaud je mets . . .
(i) Oui, je me dépêche pour aller à l'école.
Non, je ne me dépêche pas pour aller à l'école.
(j) Oui, je me dépêche pour rentrer de l'école.
Non, je ne me dépêche pas pour rentrer de l'école.

9 **(a)** Get up.
(b) Brush your teeth.
(c) Go to bed.
(d) Get up.
(e) Let's get washed.

10 **(a)** Réveille-toi.
(b) Réveillez-vous.
(c) Levons-nous.
(d) Brosse-toi les cheveux.
(e) Dépêchez-vous.

11 **(a)** Il est cinq heures du soir.
(b) Il est onze heures et demie du matin.
(c) Il est huit heures vingt du matin.
(d) Il est dix heures dix du soir.
(e) Il est onze heures vingt-cinq du soir.
(f) Il est dix heures moins le quart du soir.
(g) Il est trois heures moins vingt-cinq de l'après-midi.
(h) Il est minuit moins cinq.
(i) Il est six heures dix du matin.
(j) Il est sept heures vingt-cinq du soir.

Unit 5

2 **(a)** She likes hearing from Céline.
(b) On a farm two kilometres from Vercors.
(c) Feed the animals.
(d) Collecting the eggs.
(e) Grandfather gets angry.
(f) Swim in the river.
(g) Go fishing.
(h) Staying with the animals.
(i) A week.
(j) Send her a postcard of the Houses of Parliament.

3 **(a)** J'écris beaucoup de lettres.
(b) Ils écrivent des cartes postales.
(c) Nous écrivons à nos amis.
(d) Elle écrit à son amie.
(e) Tu écris beaucoup de lettres?
(f) Elles écrivent beaucoup de cartes postales.
(g) Vous écrivez à vos copains?
(h) Il écrit une lettre.
(i) Ils écrivent des lettres.
(j) Tu écris à tes parents?

4 **(a)** Oui, j'ai un correspondant français.
Non, je n'ai pas de correspondant français.
(b) Oui, j'ai une correspondante française.
Non, je n'ai pas de correspondante française.
(c) Oui, j'écris souvent des lettres.
Non, je n'écris pas souvent de lettres.
(d) Oui, j'écris souvent des cartes postales.
Non, je n'écris pas souvent de cartes postales.
(e) Oui, j'écris à mes grands-parents.
Non, je n'écris pas à mes grands-parents.

5 **(a)** Nous recevons des lettres de nos amis.
(b) Je reçois une lettre de ma grand'mère.
(c) Elles reçoivent des cartes postales de leurs amies.

(d) Tu reçois des cartes postales de tes amis.
(e) Ils reçoivent des cartes postales.
(f) Elle reçoit une lettre de sa copine.
(g) Vous recevez des cartes postales.
(h) Il reçoit des lettres de ses amis.
(i) Ils reçoivent des lettres de leurs parents.
(j) Je reçois des cartes postales de mes amis.

6 (a) Oui, je reçois des cartes postales de mes amis.
Non, je ne reçois pas de cartes postales de mes amis.
(b) Oui, je reçois des lettres de mes grands-parents.
Non, je ne reçois pas de lettres de mes grands-parents.
(c) Oui, je reçois souvent des lettres.
Non, je ne reçois pas souvent de lettres.
(d) Oui, il reçoit souvent des lettres.
Non, il ne reçoit pas souvent de lettres.
(e) Oui, elle reçoit souvent des cartes postales.
Non, elle ne reçoit pas souvent de cartes postales.

Unit 6

2 (a) At the post office and at the tobacconists
(b) Yellow
(c) Autres Destinations
(d) Lettres
(e) Large letters or printed matter

3 (a) In town
(b) Buying stamps
(c) She is going to send a letter to her friend Françoise.
(d) Write to each other
(e) All their friends
(f) No one
(g) His friend Frédéric
(h) Rarely
(i) An interesting stamp
(j) Collecting stamps

4 (a) Ils achètent des timbres-poste.
(b) Nous achetons des cartes postales.
(c) Tu achètes un timbre-poste?
(d) J'achète trois timbres-poste.
(e) Elles achetènt de jolis cadeaux.
(f) Il achète des timbres-poste.
(g) Vous achetez des timbres-poste en ville?
(h) Elle achète des timbres-poste au bureau de tabac.
(i) Tu achètes des cartes postales au bureau de tabac?
(j) J'achète des timbres-poste au bureau de tabac.

5 (a) Oui, j'achète des cartes postales.
Non, je n'achète pas de cartes postales.
(b) Oui, j'achète des timbres-poste.
Non, je n'achète pas de timbres-poste.
(c) Oui, j'achète des timbres-poste au bureau de tabac.
Non, je n'achète pas de timbres-poste au bureau de tabac.
(d) Oui, mon père achète des timbres-poste.
Non, mon père n'achète pas de timbres-poste.
(e) Oui, il envoie des cartes postales.
Non, il n'envoie pas de cartes postales.
(f) Oui, elle achète des timbres-poste au bureau de tabac.
Non, elle n'achète pas de timbres-poste au bureau de tabac.
(g) Oui, je préfère le téléphone.
Non, je ne préfère pas le téléphone.
(h) Oui, je collectionne les timbres-poste.
Non, je ne collectionne pas les timbres-poste.
(i) Oui, je reçois souvent des cadeaux.
Non, je ne reçois pas souvent de cadeaux.
(j) J'écris des lettres à . . .

6 (a) Il y a un bureau de poste près d'ici, s'il vous plaît?
(b) Pour aller au bureau de poste, s'il vous plaît?
(c) C'est combien pour envoyer une carte postale en Grande-Bretagne, s'il vous plaît?
(d) C'est combien pour envoyer une lettre en Grande-Bretagne, s'il vous plaît?
(e) Il y a une boîte aux lettres près d'ici, s'il vous plaît?
(f) A quelle heure est la dernière levée?
(g) Yes, over there on the right.
(h) Take the second street on the left.
(i) One franc seventy.
(j) Two francs forty.
(k) Yes, over there opposite the bank.
(l) At half past six in the evening.

Unit 7

2 (a) (ii)
(b) (iv)
(c) (i)
(d) (iii)
(e) (ii)
(f) (i)
(g) (ii)
(h) (iv)
(i) (i)
(j) (iv)

3 8 huit
16 seize
21 vingt et un

39 trente-neuf
54 cinquante-quatre
77 soixante-dix-sept
84 quatre-vingt-quatre
93 quatre-vingt-treize
99 quatre-vingt-dix-neuf
100 cent

4 500 cinq cents
436 quatre cent trente-six
728 sept cent vingt-huit
4,000 quatre mille
3,000,000 trois millions

5 (a) le premier jour
   (b) le dernier car
   (c) la quatrième rue
   (d) la troisième maison
   (e) le cinq juin

6 (a) Nous prenons l'autobus.
   (b) Ils prennent l'autobus.
   (c) Elle prend la première rue à droite.
   (d) Tu prends la deuxième rue à droite.
   (e) Elle prennent la troisième rue à gauche.
   (f) Je prends le train.
   (g) Vous prenez le train?
   (h) Il prend ses livres.
   (i) Je prends un café.
   (j) Elles prennent des glaces.

7 (a) Prends la première rue à droite.
   (b) Prenons l'autobus.
   (c) Prenez la deuxième rue à gauche.
   (d) Réveille-toi.
   (e) Allons en ville.

Unit 8

1 Learning: e.g. Je prends les crudités, une
   omelette au jambon, des pommes frites et une
   glace.

2 (a) The tenth of March.
   (b) It is Céline's birthday.
   (c) In a restaurant.
   (d) A ham omelette with beans.
   (e) Roast chicken.
   (f) Beans.
   (g) Inside the restaurant.
   (h) She is hot.
   (i) Outside.
   (j) On the left, outside.

3 (a) Nous voulons manger au restaurant.
   (b) Ils veulent manger à la terrasse.
   (c) Je veux fêter mon anniversaire au
   restaurant.

   (d) Tu peux venir?
   (e) Vous voulez venir?
   (f) Elles peuvent aller au cinéma.
   (g) Tu veux de la salade?
   (h) Il peut fêter son anniversaire au restaurant.
   (i) Elle veut se mettre à la terrasse.
   (j) On peut manger au restaurant.

4 (a) Je sais préparer une omelette.
   (b) Vous savez préparer une omelette?
   (c) Elle sait préparer une omelette au jambon.
   (d) Tu sais faire la cuisine?
   (e) Ils savent préparer une salade de tomates.

5 3 (a) We wish to eat in the restaurant.
     (b) They want to eat outside (the restaurant).
     (c) I want to celebrate my birthday at the
     restaurant.
     (d) Can you come?
     (e) Do you want to come?
     (f) They can go to the cinema.
     (g) Do you want any salad?
     (h) He can celebrate his birthday at the
     restaurant.
     (i) She wants to sit outside.
     (j) One (We) can eat at the restaurant.
   4 (a) I know how to make an omelette.
     (b) Do you know how to make an omelette?
     (c) She knows how to make a ham omelette.
     (d) Can you cook? (Do you know how to cook?)
     (e) They know how to make a tomato salad.

6 (a) e.g. J'aime le melon; j'aime le jambon;
              j'aime les petits pois; j'aime les crêpes.
   (b) e.g. Je n'aime pas le potage; je n'aime pas
              les rognons; je n'aime pas les carottes;
              je n'aime pas les pâtisseries.

7 (a) Une table pour cinq (personnes), s'il vous
   plaît.
   (b) Nous pouvons nous mettre à la terrasse?
   (c) Je voudrais voir le menu.
   (d) Qu'est-ce que vous voulez prendre?
   (e) Tu as froid, maman?
   (f) Je voudrais du potage, un steak (bifteck), des
   frites et une glace, s'il vous plaît.
   (g) L'addition, s'il vous plaît.
   (h) Le service est compris?

Unit 9

2 (a) J'ai . . frère(s)
       Je n'ai pas de frères.
   (b) J'ai . . . soeur(s).
       Je n'ai pas de soeurs.
   (c) Oui, j'ai . . neveu(x)
       Non, je n'ai pas de neveux.

(d) Oui, j'ai . . . nièce(s).
Non je n'ai pas de nièce(s).
(e) J'ai . . . cousin(s).
Je n'ai pas de cousins
(f) J'ai . . . cousine(s)
Je n'ai pas de cousines.

3 **(a)** Je te présente ma mère.
(b) Je vous présente ma mère.
(c) Je vous présente mon frère.
(d) Je te présente mon frère.
(e) Je te présente ma soeur.
(f) Je vous présente ma tante.
(g) Je vous présente mon oncle.
(h) Je te présente ma grand'mère.
(i) Je te présente mon grand-père.
(j) Je vous présente ma cousine.

5 **(a)** Ils connaissent mon père.
(b) Je connais son père.
(c) Vous connaissez ma mère?
(d) Elle connaît ma soeur.
(e) Tu connais mes grands-parents?
(f) Elles connaissent ma tante.
(g) Il connaît mon oncle.
(h) Nous connaissons vos cousins.
(i) Elle connaît votre nièce.
(j) Ils connaissent ton grand-père.

6 **(a)** Tu connais mon père?
(b) Vous connaissez ma mère?
(c) Tu connais mon frère?
(d) Tu connais ma soeur?
(e) Vous connaissez mon oncle?

7 **(a)** Bonjour, Marc.
(b) Bonjour, Céline.
(c) Enchanté(e), monsieur.
(d) Enchanté(e), madame.
(e) Enchanté(e), monsieur.
(f) Enchanté(e), madame.
(g) Enchanté(e), madame.
(h) Enchanté(e), monsieur.
(i) Enchanté(e), monsieur.
(j) Enchanté(e), madame.

8 **(a)** Donnez-moi une glace au chocolat, s'il vous plaît.
(b) Je voudrais un steak et des frites, s'il vous plaît.
(c) Un litre de lait, s'il vous plaît.
(d) Voulez-vous me passer le sel?
(e) Tu peux (vous pouvez) me passer le pain, s'il te (vous) plaît?

9 **(a)** Oh, pardon, monsieur.
(b) Il n'y a pas de mal.
(c) Je regrette d'être en retard.
(d) Ça ne fait rien.
(e) Je suis désolé(e), madame.

Unit 10

4 **(a)** Je suis souffrant(e).
(b) Tu es malade?
(c) Il faut consulter un médecin.
(d) Comment vas-tu?
(e) Je suis malade.
(f) J'ai mal à la tête.
(g) J'ai mal au dos.
(h) J'ai mal à l'oreille.
(i) Vous êtes souffrant(e)?
(j) Vous êtes malade?

5 **(a)** J'ai de la fièvre.
(b) J'ai mal à la gorge.

7 **(a)** Sunburn
(b) To the chemist's
(c) A cream
(d) To apply it three times a day

8 **(a)** **(i)** Bonjour, monsieur.
(ii) J'ai une crise de foie.
(iii) Pouvez-vous me prescrire quelque chose?
(iv) C'est combien?
(b) **(i)** How old are you?
(ii) Do you hurt anywhere else?
(iii) Do you have diarrhoea?
(iv) Do you have any allergies?
(c) He has recommended some tablets. One tablet is to be taken in a glass of water every four hours.

9 **(a)** un oeil
(b) les yeux
(c) le pied
(d) la bouche
(e) une oreille
(f) la jambe
(g) le genou
(h) le nez
(i) le bras
(j) une épaule
(k) Je suis souffrant(e)
(l) Je suis malade.
(m) Il faut consulter un médecin.
(n) J'ai mal à la tête.
(o) J'ai une crise de foie.
(p) Comment vas-tu?
(q) Comment allez-vous?
(r) J'ai un coup de soleil.
(s) J'ai de la fièvre.
(t) Je suis enrhumé(e).

Unit 11

2 (a) Some brochures, a list of the hotels, and a plan of the town.
(b) The address of the zoo at Rennes.
(c) She requires information about the animals in the zoo.
(d) A project.
(e) Her biology teacher.

---

3 (Your name)   Monsieur le Directeur
(Your address)   du Syndicat
                  d'Initiative
           La Rochelle

Monsieur,
      Je vous prie de m'envoyer des informations sur la ville de La Rochelle. Voulez-vous m'envoyer une liste des hôtels, une liste des campings de la région, et des informations sur les événements à venir.
      Avec mes remerciements anticipés, je vous prie d'agréer, Monsieur, l'expression de mes sentiments distingués.

---

4 (a) Hotels and guided visits in La Rochelle
(b) Which one is the best hotel.
(c) Le Yachtman
(d) On the Valin quay
(e) A plan of the town

5 (a) Quels sports? Which sports?
(b) Quels événements à venir? Which coming events?
(c) Quelles promenades? Which walks?
(d) Quelle ville? Which town?
(e) Quels spectacles? Which shows?
(f) Quel film? Which film?
(g) Quels campings? Which campsites?
(h) Quelles spécialités de la région?
    Which regional specialities?
(i) Quel travail de recherches? Which project?
(j) Quel quai? Which quay?

6 (a) Il me faut un plan de la ville.
    J'ai besoin d'un plan de la ville.
(b) Il me faut des informations sur la ville de Rennes.
    J'ai besoin des informations sur la ville de Rennes.
(c) Il me faut des brochures.
    J'ai besoin des brochures.
(d) Il me faut une liste des restaurants.
    J'ai besoin d'une liste des restaurants.
(e) Il me faut des informations sur les événements à venir.
    J'ai besoin des informations sur les événements à venir.

7 (a) From 12 noon until 2 p.m.
(b) Sunday mornings and all day on Mondays
(c) 3 francs
(d) Nothing
(e) On Tuesdays

Unit 12

1 (a) A quelle heure part le prochain car pour Paris?
(b) A quelle heure part le premier (auto) bus pour Vincennes?
(c) A quelle heure part le dernier ferry?
(d) A quelle heure part le prochain ferry?
(e) A quelle heure arrive le prochain train?
(f) A quelle heure arrive le prochain avion?
(g) A quelle heure part le prochain hovercraft?
(h) A quelle heure part le dernier train?
(i) A quelle heure part le prochain train pour Lyon?
(j) A quelle heure part le mini-bus?

2 (a) The next coach for Paris leaves at two o'clock in the afternoon.
(b) The first bus for Vincennes leaves at half past five.
(c) The last ferry leaves at eleven in the evening.
(d) The next ferry leaves at a quarter past eleven.
(e) The next train arrives at four o'clock in the afternoon.
(f) The next plane arrives at three o'clock in the afternoon.
(g) The next hovercraft leaves at seven o'clock in the evening.
(h) The last train leaves at ten o'clock in the evening.
(i) The next train for Lyon leaves at half past ten.
(j) The mini-bus leaves at six o'clock in the evening.

3 (a) Le prochain car part à dix heures.
(b) Nous partons à neuf heures et demie.
(c) Tu pars à huit heures?
(d) Elles partent à midi.
(e) Vous partez à six heures?
(f) Le premier train part à vingt heures.
(g) Il part à vingt heures.
(h) Je pars pour Paris.
(i) Elle part pour Lyon.
(j) Ils partent à cinq heures moins le quart.

4 (a) He wants to know if there is a bus-station nearby.
(b) A hundred metres away.

(c) On the right.
(d) If there are any coaches for Toulouse that afternoon.
(e) Yes. There is one at five o'clock.

5 (a) C'est loin la gare?
(b) A quelle distance se trouve la gare, s'il vous plaît?
(c) C'est loin, l'arrêt d'autobus?
(d) A quelle distance se trouve l'arrêt d'autobus, s'il vous plaît?
(e) C'est loin, l'aéroport?
(f) A quelle distance se trouve l'aéroport, s'il vous plaît?
(g) C'est loin, l' hoverport?
(h) A quelle distance se trouve l' hoverport, s'il vous plaît?
(i) C'est loin, la station de métro?
(j) A quelle distance se trouve la station de métro, s'il vous plaît?

6 (a) No, fifty metres from here.
(b) Fifty metres from here.
(c) No, thirty metres from here.
(d) Thirty metres from here.
(e) No, two kilometres from here.
(f) Two kilometres from here.
(g) No, one kilometre from here.
(h) One kilometre from here.
(i) No, a hundred metres from here.
(j) A hundred metres from here.

7 (a) Le premier car de Rémuzat part à six heures et quart du matin.
(b) Le premier car de Nyons part à sept heures du matin.
(c) Le dernier car de Nyons part à sept heures du soir.
(d) Le dernier car d'Orange part à huit heures et demie du soir.
(e) Le premier car d'Orange part à huit heures et demie du matin.
(f) Il arrive à Avignon à neuf heures quinze.
(g) Il arrive à Avignon à quinze heures quinze.
(h) Il arrive à Avignon à vingt et une heures quinze.

8 Tickets can be booked for travel abroad. Plane tickets can be booked but railway tickets are usually booked at the railway station.

Unit 13

2 (a) To Belfort
(b) At half past three in the afternoon
(c) No
(d) The traveller must change at Dijon.
(e) Platform seven

(f) On the right
(g) No
(h) On the left

3 (a) Il y a un train pour Bordeaux ce matin?
(b) C'est un train direct?
(c) De quelle voie part le train pour Bordeaux?
(d) Faut-il réserver une place?
(e) Où se trouve la salle d'attente, s'il vous plaît?

5 (a) To Nancy
(b) A single ticket
(c) First class
(d) He wants to reserve a seat
(e) Today
(f) At midday
(g) 120 francs
About £9

6 (a) Un aller simple pour Paris, s'il vous plaît.
(b) De deuxième classe
(c) Un aller et retour pour Paris, s'il vous plaît.
(d) De première classe
(e) Je voudrais réserver une place.

7 (a) Il les achète.
(b) Il l'achète.
(c) Je la réserve.
(d) Nous les réservons.
(e) Nous le voyons.
(f) Elle l'attend.
(g) Vous l'attendez.
(h) Le voici.
(i) La voilà.
(j) La voici.

8 (a) Je te vois.
(b) Je vous vois.
(c) Il nous voit.
(d) Elle nous voit.
(e) Nous vous voyons.

Unit 14

2 (a) To passport control
(b) To passport control
(c) Give your passport to the passport officer.
(d) How long are you going to stay (in France)? Are you travelling alone?
(e) Through Customs
(f) Show your luggage.
(g) Contraband
(h) Cigarettes, perfume, alcohol
(i) It is a present for his penfriend's parents.
(j) He doesn't smoke.

3 (a) Elle ouvre la valise.
(b) Ils ouvrent les passeports.
(c) J'ouvre mon passeport.

114

(d) Tu ouvres ton sac à main.
(e) Vous ouvrez votre valise.
(f) Elles ouvrent leurs valises.
(g) Elle ouvre son sac à main.
(h) Il ouvre son sac à dos.
(i) Nous ouvrons nos valises.
(j) J'ouvre ma valise.

4 (a) Le touriste lui montre le passeport.
(b) Il lui montre la valise.
(c) Elle leur montre ses valises.
(d) Elle lui montre son passeport.
(e) Il leur offre une bouteille de whisky.

5 (a) Mettez-le sur le comptoir.
(b) Mettez-les sur le comptoir.
(c) Montrez-le-moi.
(d) Montrez-les-moi.
(e) Ouvrez-le.
(f) Ouvrez-la.
(g) Dépêche-toi.
(h) Lève-toi.
(i) Mettons-nous à la terrasse.
(j) Écrivons-nous.

6 (a) Le voici, monsieur.
(b) J'ai ...ans.
(c) Trois semaines, monsieur.
(d) A Royan.
(e) Chez mon/ma correspondant(e).
(f) Oui, monsieur.

7 (a) Les voici, monsieur.
(b) J'ai une valise et un sac à dos.
(c) Non, je n'ai rien à déclarer.
(d) Non, monsieur.
(e) Je n'ai pas de cigarettes mais j'ai une petite bouteille de parfum. C'est un cadeau pour la mère de mon/ma correspondant(e).

Unit 15

1 (a) Geography
(b) Canada
(c) Visit her friend in Canada.
(d) Studying a map of the world.
(e) She thinks that it is the most beautiful country in the world.
(f) She thinks that it is even more beautiful than France.

3 (a) Madrid est la capitale de l'Espagne.
(b) Berne est la capitale de la Suisse.
(c) Bruxelles est la capitale de la Belgique.
(d) Edimbourg est la capitale de l'Écosse.
(e) Cardiff est la capitale du Pays de Galles.
(f) Londres est la capitale de l'Angleterre.
(g) Bonn est la capitale de l'Allemagne.
(h) Amsterdam est la capitale des Pays Bas.

(i) Copenhague est la capitale du Danemark.
(j) Rome est la capitale de l'Italie.

4 (a) Le Canada est plus grand que la France.
(b) Le Japon est plus petit que la Russie.
(c) Le Pays de Galles est aussi vert que l'Irlande.
(d) Le Portugal est moins vert que l'Écosse.
(e) La Sardaigne est aussi belle que la Corse.

5 (a) Elle habite l'Écosse.
(b) Il habite l'Irlande.
(c) Il habite l'Espagne.
(d) Elle habite les Pays Bas.
(e) Elle habite la Belgique.
(f) Elle habite le Danemark.
(g) Il habite la Chine.
(h) Il habite le Luxembourg.
(i) Elle habite la Nouvelle Zélande.
(j) Il habite la Russie.

6 (a) Le géographie est la matière la plus facile.
(b) La biologie est la matière la plus difficile.
(c) Marc et Céline sont les enfants les plus intelligents.
(d) Marc est l'enfant le plus amusant.
(e) Quelqufois c'est l'enfant le plus ennuyeux.
(f) Marc est le plus jeune élève de sa classe.
(g) La France est le plus beau pays d'Europe.
(h) La Corse est la plus belle île de la Méditerranée.
(i) Céline est la meilleure élève de sa classe.
(j) Frédéric est le meilleur élève de sa classe.

7 Personal choice answers.

Unit 16

1 (a) At the edge of the pavement.
(b) He has been knocked down by a cyclist and has hurt his foot.
(c) A police station
(d) Get a policeman.
(e) Help the boy to a bench nearby.

2 (a) Qu'est-ce qu'il a?
(b) Qu'est-ce que tu as?
(c) Qu'est-ce qu'elle a?
(d) Qu'est-ce qu'ils ont?
(e) Qu'est-ce qu'il y a?

3 (a) J'ai mal à la jambe.
Ma jambe me fait mal.
(b) J'ai mal à la tête.
Ma tête me fait mal.
(c) J'ai mal à l'oreille.
Mon oreille me fait mal.
(d) J'ai mal au genou.
Mon genou me fait mal.
(e) J'ai mal au bras.
Mon bras me fait mal.

4 (a) Va chercher mon professeur.
  (b) Va chercher ma mère.
  (c) Allez chercher mon père.
  (d) Allez chercher un agent (de police).
  (e) Allez chercher un médecin.

5 (a) On a chair
  (b) Next to him
  (c) The injured foot
  (d) Call a doctor to attend to him
  (e) Telephone the boy's mother

6 (a) Je m'assieds.
  (b) Je suis assis(e).
  (c) Elles sont assises.
  (d) Ils s'asseyent.
  (e) Il s'assied.
  (f) Elle est assise.
  (g) Nous nous asseyons.
  (h) Asseyons-nous.
  (i) Assieds-toi.
  (j) Asseyez-vous.

7 (a) Qu'est-ce qu'il y a?
  (b) Il faut appeler la police.
  (c) Il faut appeler un médecin.
  (d) Il faut appeler une ambulance.
  (e) Au secours!

8 (a) Fire!
  (b) We must call the fire-brigade.
  (c) A child has been injured.
  (d) We must telephone the hospital.
  (e) Your name and your address, please.

9 (a) Le pied blessé
  (b) La tête blessée
  (c) Les mains brûlées
  (d) Les pieds brûlés
  (e) Le poignet cassé
  (f) La jambe cassée
  (g) Le doigt coupé
  (h) Le nez coupé
  (i) Le poignet foulé
  (j) La cheville foulée

Unit 17

1 (a) J'ai marché/vous avez marché/ils ont marché
  (b) J'ai traversé/vous avez traversé/ils ont traversé
  (c) J'ai acheté/vous avez acheté/ils ont acheté
  (d) J'ai visité/vous avez visité/ils ont visité
  (e) J'ai oublié/vous avez oublié/ils ont oublié
  (f) J'ai choisi/vous avez choisi/ils ont choisi
  (g) J'ai averti/vous avez averti/ils ont averti
  (h) J'ai vendu/vous avez vendu/ils ont vendu
  (i) J'ai rencontré/vous avez rencontré/ils ont rencontré

(j) J'ai répondu/vous avez répondu/ils ont répondu

2 (a) I/you/they/walked (have walked)
  (b) I/you/they/crossed (have crossed)
  (c) I/you/they/bought (have bought)
  (d) I/you/they/visited (have visited)
  (e) I/you/they/forgot (have forgotten)
  (f) I/you/they/chose (have chosen)
  (g) I/you/they/warned (have warned) also notified (have notified)
  (h) I/you/they/sold (have sold)
  (i) I/you/they/met (have met)
  (j) I/you/they/replied (have replied)

4 (a) (iv)
  (b) (ii)
  (c) (iii)
  (d) (i)
  (e) (iii)
  (f) (iv)
  (g) (iv)
  (h) (i)
  (i) (ii)
  (j) (i)

5 (a) J'y vais.
  (b) Nous y allons.
  (c) Elle y a perdu son porte-monnaie.
  (d) Allons-y.
  (e) Allez-y.
  (f) J'aime y aller.
  (g) Elle aime y faire ses courses.
  (h) J'y ai perdu mon porte-monnaie.
  (i) Allez-y.
  (j) Elles y vont.

6 J'ai décidé d'aller en ville pour faire des courses. J'ai attendu l'autobus au coin de la rue. J'y ai rencontré mes amis. Nous avons marché le long de la rue du Commerce: Nous avons regardé les vitrines des grands magasins. J'ai préféré les petites boutiques mais mes amis ont préféré les grands magasins. J'ai acheté des provisions pour ma mère mais j'ai laissé tomber mon sac à main. Mon ami Paul a ramassé mon porte-monnaie.

Unit 18

1 (a) Elles ont fait des achats.
  (b) Nous avons dit bonjour.
  (c) Ils ont voulu aller en ville.
  (d) J'ai pris le chariot.
  (e) Vous avez mis les provisions dans le panier.
  (f) Il a eu un accident.
  (g) Elle a écrit une liste.
  (h) Tu as pu porter toutes les provisions?
  (i) J'ai compris.
  (j) Nous avons vu nos amis.

2 (a) Elle a fait ses achats mercredi dernier.
   (b) Elle a fait ses achats au supermarché.
   (c) Elle a poussé un chariot.
   (d) La famille Gavarin aime bien manger.
   (e) Elle n'a pas pu trouver sa confiture favorite.
   (f) La vendeuse a indiqué le rayon à gauche.
   (g) Elle s'appelle Madame Gérard.
   (h) Devant le rayon des fromages.
   (i) Madame Gérard.
   (j) Elle doit téléphoner à son mari.
   (k) Parce qu'elle a oublié ce que son mari lui a demandé d'acheter.
   (l) Madame Gérard est distraite.
   (m) Madame Gavarin est distraite aussi.
   (n) Elle a mis ses pantoufles.
   (o) Son mari n'a pas voulu l'accompagner.
   (p) Madame Gavarin a beaucoup à faire.
   (q) Monsieur Gavarin déteste faire les achats.
   (r) Ce qu'ils vont manger ce soir.
   (s) La famille a mangé du porc.
   (t) Les enfants préfèrent le bifteck.

3 (a) J'ai voulu acheter un carnet.
   (b) J'ai voulu acheter une gomme.
   (c) J'ai voulu acheter un stylo.
   (d) J'ai voulu acheter un cahier.
   (e) J'ai voulu acheter un disque.

4 (a) J'ai dû acheter du porc pour ma mère.
   (b) J'ai dû acheter du fromage pour ma mère.
   (c) J'ai dû acheter des boîtes de conserves pour ma mère.
   (d) J'ai dû acheter du pain pour ma mère.
   (e) J'ai dû acheter un kilo de pommes de terre pour ma mère.

5 (a) J'y ai vu mon professeur.
   (b) J'y ai vu mon ami(e).
   (c) J'y ai vu ma soeur.
   (d) J'y ai vu mon docteur.
   (e) J'y ai vu ma cousine.

6 (a) Oui, j'en ai acheté.
   (b) Oui, j'en ai acheté.
   (c) Oui, j'en ai acheté.
   (d) Oui, j'en ai acheté.
   (e) Oui, j'en ai acheté.
   (f) Oui, j'en ai acheté deux.
   (g) Oui, j'en ai acheté trois.
   (h) Oui, j'en ai acheté un kilo.
   (i) Oui, j'en ai acheté un demi-kilo.
   (j) Oui, j'en ai acheté deux cents grammes.

7 (a) one hundred and sixty-two francs and fifteen centimes
   (b) ninety-seven francs and twenty centimes
   (c) seventy-six francs and seventy-eight centimes
   (d) two hundred and forty-nine francs and twelve centimes
   (e) fifty-three francs and ninety-one centimes

Unit 19

2 (a) He did do-it-yourself jobs.
   (b) He didn't do the gardening.
   (c) She knitted.
   (d) She didn't watch television.
   (e) She did her homework.
   (f) She didn't watch television.
   (g) He watched television.
   (h) He didn't do his homework.

3 (a) Madame Gavarin n'a pas voulu sortir.
   (b) Marc n'a pas fait ses devoirs.
   (c) Monsieur Gavarin n'a pas aidé sa femme.
   (d) Céline n'a pas écrit une lettre.
   (e) Nous n'avons pas pu sortir.
   (f) Tu n'as pas vu tes copains.
   (g) Ils n'ont pas collectionné les timbres-poste.
   (h) Je n'ai pas été amateur de cinéma.
   (i) Vous n'avez pas pris de photos.
   (j) Elles n'ont pas collectionné les posters.

4 Personal choice answers.
   (a) Oui, j'aime le sport/Je déteste le sport.
   (b) Je préfère . . .
   (c) Oui, je joue de (de la) . . .
   (d) Je joue du (de la) . . .
   (e) Oui, je collectionne les timbres-poste.
       Non, je ne collectionne pas les timbres-poste.
   (f) Oui, je collectionne les posters.
       Non, je ne collectionne pas les posters.
   (g) Je ne peux pas supporter . . .
   (h) Oui, je les aime.
       Non, je ne les aime pas.
   (i) J'aime . . .
   (j) Oui, j'aime les écouter.
       Non, je n'aime pas les écouter.

5 (a) Tu collectionnnes les disques?
   (b) Tu aimes nager?
   (c) Tu joues au football?
   (d) Tu joues du violon?
   (e) Tu aimes regarder la télévision?
   (f) Tu aimes construire des maquettes?
   (g) Tu aimes faire le jardinage?
   (h) Tu préfères regarder la télévision?
   (i) Tu aimes danser?
   (j) Tu fais du judo?

8 (a) Mon frère/ma soeur a écouté des disques.
   (b) Il/elle n'a pas regardé la télévision.
   (c) Il/elle collectionne les timbres-poste.
   (d) Il/elle ne peut pas supporter les devoirs.
   (e) Il/elle adore le sport.

Unit 20

1 (a) Ils ont passé l'après-midi au centre sportif.
 (b) Ils y ont rencontré leurs camarades Frédéric et Françoise.
 (c) Elles ont décidé de jouer au squash.
 (d) Elle a oublié sa raquette.
 (e) Elle l'a laissée sur la table de la cuisine.
 (f) Marc l'a vue.
 (g) Elles ont retenu une place.
 (h) Françoise à gagné le premier match.
 (i) Ils ont joué trois matchs.
 (j) Marc a gagné un match seulement.

2 (a) Oui, je l'ai laissé à la maison.
 (b) Oui, je l'ai laissée à la maison.
 (c) Oui, je les ai laissés à la maison.
 (d) Oui, je l'ai laissé à la maison.
 (e) Oui, je les ai laissées à la maison.

3 (a) Combien de livres as-tu achetés?
 (b) Combien de matchs as-tu gagnés?
 (c) Combien de boîtes as-tu achetées?
 (d) Combien d'enfants as-tu vus?
 (e) Combien de cartes postales as-tu achetées?

4 (a) Où est la raquette que j'ai achetée?
 (b) Où sont les chaussures que j'ai achetées?
 (c) Où est le journal que j'ai acheté?
 (d) Il nous a vus en ville.
 (e) Elle m'a vu en ville.
 (f) J'ai gagné deux matchs.
 (g) J'ai laissé ma raquette à la maison.
 (h) Je l'ai laissée à la maison.
 (i) J'ai vu mes amies.
 (j) Je les ai vues.

5 (a) Pour aller au Syndicat d'Initiative, s'il vous plaît?
 (b) Pour aller au centre sportif, s'il vous plaît?
 (c) C'est loin?
 (d) Y a-t-il un centre sportif près d'ici, s'il vous plaît?
 (e) Il faut prendre l'autobus?

6 (a) Go straight on then turn left after the baker's.
 (b) You must catch the bus in front of the Tourist Office. Route (line) three.
 (c) Yes, two kilometres from here.
 (d) Yes, a hundred metres away.
 (e) No, you can get there on foot.

7 (a) Allez jusqu'au rond-point puis tournez à droite.
 (b) Prenez la troisième rue à droite.
 (c) Allez jusqu'au rond-point puis tournez à gauche.
 (d) Prenez la deuxième rue à gauche.
 (e) Allez au rond-point puis continuez tout droit.

Unit 21

2 (a) Monsieur Gavarin est allé à la station-service.
 (b) Les enfants sont descendus de la voiture.
 (c) Je suis resté(e) à la maison.
 (d) Vous êtes venu(e)(s) à pied.
 (e) Nous sommes parti(e)s à huit heures.
 (f) Madame Gavarin est sortie de la maison.
 (g) Tu es arrivé(e) à neuf heures et demie.
 (h) Elles sont devenues fatiguées
 (i) Elle est entrée dans le magasin.
 (j) Ils sont retournés à la maison.

3 (a) Mr Gavarin went to the service-station.
 (b) The children got out of the car.
 (c) I stayed at home.
 (d) You came on foot.
 (e) We left at eight o'clock.
 (f) Mrs Gavarin went out of the house.
 (g) You arrived at half past nine.
 (h) They became tired.
 (i) She went into the shop.
 (j) They returned home.

4 (a) (iv)
 (b) (i)
 (c) (iii)
 (d) (iii)
 (e) (i)
 (f) (iii)
 (g) (iv)
 (h) (ii)
 (i) (iv)
 (j) (ii)

5 (a) C'est libre-service?
 (b) Voulez-vous faire le plein d'essence, s'il vous plaît?
 (c) Voulez-vous vérifier le niveau d'huile, s'il vous plaît?
 (d) Voulez-vous vérifier le niveau d'eau, s'il vous plaît?
 (e) Ça fait combien?

6 (a) No, it isn't self-service.
 (b) Shall I fill up with petrol?
 (c) You need oil.
 (d) You need water.
 (e) That's one hundred and twenty francs.

Unit 22

2 (a) (ii)
 (b) (i)
 (c) (iii)
 (d) (iv)
 (e) (iv)

(f) (iii)
(g) (i)
(h) (ii)
(i) (iii)
(j) (iv)

5 **(a)** Oui, j'aime/Non, je n'aime pas l'école.
(b) Je suis en. . . .
(c) Oui, j'aime/Non, je n'aime pas les maths.
(d) Oui, j'aime/Non, je n'aime pas le français.
(e) Oui, je suis/Non, je ne suis pas fort(e) en maths.
(f) Oui, je suis/Non, je ne suis pas faible en anglais.
(g) C'est . . .
(h) Il y en a . . .
(i) Il/elle s'appelle . . .
(j) Oui, j'aime/Non, je n'aime pas la gymnastique.

6 **(a)** Tu aimes l'école?
(b) Tu es en quelle classe?
(c) Tu aimes l'anglais?
(d) Tu es fort(e) en anglais?
(e) Tu aimes la physique?
(f) Quelle est ta matière préférée?
(g) Combien de professeurs y a-t-il dans ton école?
(h) Tu aimes le sport?
(i) Tu vas à l'ècole le samedi matin?
(j) Tu vas à l'école le mercredi après-midi?

Unit 23

1 **(a)** Elle se trouve dans la rue principale de Valréas.
(b) Il veut acheter un journal anglais.
(c) Il a stationné sa voiture sur la Place de la Poste.
(d) Non, il ne sait pas où se trouve la maison de la presse.
(e) Devant lui il y a le bureau de poste.
(f) Derrière lui il y a un café.
(g) Il est allé au café.
(h) Il y est resté une demi-heure.
(i) Non, elle se trouve en face de l'église.
(j) Le touriste s'est trompé.

2 **(a)** Pour moi
(b) Pour eux
(c) Devant nous
(d) Devant vous
(e) A côté de lui
(f) En face de vous
(g) Près de moi
(h) Pour elles
(i) Derrière toi
(j) Chez elle

3 **(a)** On peut y acheter les quotidiens, les magazines, les revues, les livres et la papeterie.
(b) On les voit souvent dans les grandes villes.
(c) On y vend aussi les cartes et les cartes postales.
(d) On peut y trouver en été des journaux étrangers.
(e) Les journaux les mieux connus en France sont *Le Figaro* et *Le Monde*.
(f) Il s'appelle *Le Progrès*!
(g) Un des magazines les plus populaires en France c'est *Paris Match*.
(h) *Salut* et *Hit Parade* sont des magazines pour les jeunes au sujet de la musique pop.
(i) Pour les plus jeunes il y a *Tintin*, *Lucky Luke* et *Astérix*.
(j) Oui, j'aime/Non, je n'aime pas les bandes dessinées.

4 **(a)** Avez-vous des journaux anglais?
(b) C'est combien?
(c) Avez-vous une carte de la région?
(d) Avez-vous des cartes postales?
(e) Quels magazines avez-vous pour les jeunes?

5 **(a)** At half past nine in the evening
(b) 4 hours a day
(c) 3
(d) From the age of 7 to 77
(e) From 9 in the morning to 6 in the evening

Unit 24

1 **(a)** Yes
(b) No
(c) He wants to know exactly when and where it was lost. He also wants to know the make of camera.
(d) Monsieur,
J'accuse réception de votre lettre du 2 septembre. J'ai perdu mon appareil, un Kodak, le 15 août sur la place de la Concorde.
En attendant de vous lire, veuillez agréer, monsieur, l'expression de mes sentiments distingués.

2 **(a)** Oui, monsieur, j'ai perdu mon appareil.
(b) Je l'ai perdu près de l'église.
(c) Je l'ai perdu ce matin.
(d) C'est un Agfa.
(e) Merci, monsieur. Au revoir.

3 You must go down this street then turn right at the traffic lights. The Lost Property Office is next to the Tourist Information Office.

4 (a) Je dois aller à la banque.
   (b) Je dois aller au bureau de poste.
   (c) Nous devons aller à la pharmacie.
   (d) Nous devons aller à la gare.
   (e) Je dois aller au Syndicat d'Initiative.

5 (a) Il faut descendre cette rue.
   (b) Il faut tourner à gauche aux feux.
   (c) Il faut traverser le pont.
   (d) Il faut attraper l'autobus.
   (e) Il faut aller jusqu'au rond-point.

6 (a) Bonjour, monsieur.
   (b) J'ai perdu ma montre.
   (c) Je l'ai perdue hier.
   (d) Je l'ai perdue au jardin public.
   (e) C'est une montre digitale.

7 (a) Two weeks
   (b) In the toilet block
   (c) On the 30th of August
   (d) 10 days
   (e) The fact that it was clean and well-kept
   (f) The play areas
   (g) They thought that it had a limited choice.
   (h) To buy provisions
   (i) She thought that they were too near the dustbins.
   (j) Return to the same campsite

8 Monsieur,

En rentrant chez nous après quatre semaines de vacances, ma mère m'a dit qu'elle a laissé sa montre dans les lavabos de votre camping. Nous avons quitté le camping le 2 septembre et ma mère a perdu sa montre ce matin-là. Si vous l'avez trouvée, je vous serai reconnaissant de bien vouloir me l'envoyer.

Nous sommes restés trois semaines au camping, mais nous ne l'avons pas trouvé propre ni* bien entretenu. Heureusement, il y a un grand choix de provisions au libre-service et nous n'avons pas dû aller en ville pour faire les courses.

Nous avons bien apprécié la piscine mais elle est trop près du restaurant. Néanmoins tout le monde s'est bien amusé et nous avons l'intention d'y retourner l'année prochaine.

En attendant votre réponse, je vous prie d'agréer, Monsieur, l'expression de mes sentiments distingués.

* **ni** nor

9 Personal choice. The following are possible answers.
   (a) C'est ennuyeux.
   (b) C'est superbe.
   (c) C'est casse-pieds.
   (d) C'est chouette.
   (e) Sensas.

Unit 25

2 (a) Bonjour, madame. Je voudrais toucher un chèque de voyage.
   (b) Quel guichet, s'il vous plaît?
   (c) Combien vaut la livre sterling aujourd'hui?
   (d) J'ai mon passeport.
   (e) Il faut signer?
   (f) C'est où, la caisse?
   (g) Merci, madame. Au revoir.

3 (a) Go to the counter over there, on the left.
   (b) Eleven francs forty.
   (c) You must sign there.
   (d) The cash-desk is on the right.
   (e) Do you have your passport?

4 (a) 113 francs
   (b) 56 francs 50 (centimes)
   (c) 226 francs
   (d) 282 francs 50 (centimes)
   (e) 169 francs 60 (centimes)

5 (a) 26 April 1984
   (b) £100 in travellers' cheques
   (c) £1 – 11 francs 50(53)
   (d) (i) 7 francs 50
       (ii) about 70 pence
   (e) (i) 1,143 francs 03
       (ii) about £99.30

6 (a) Le vingt-six avril dix-neuf cent quatre-vingt-quatre.
   (b) Cent livres en chèques de voyage.
   (c) Une livre vaut onze francs cinquante à peu près* (* approx)
   (d) (i) sept francs cinquante (ii) soixante-dix pence à peu près
   (e) (i) mille cent quarante-trois francs trois
       (ii) quatre-vingt-dix-neuf livres trente pence à peu près

Glossary

Adjective This is a word which describes a noun or pronoun. It gives information about colour, size, type, etc.
e.g. l'enfant **intelligent**

Auxiliary verbs These are the verbs 'avoir' and 'être' which are used with other verbs to form the Perfect tense.

Consonants These are the letters of the alphabet other than vowels.

First person When this refers to a verb, it means 'je'

Infinitives That part of the verb which means 'To . . .'.
e.g. **aller**   to go
      avoir   to have

Irregular verbs Those verbs which do not follow the set patterns.

Negative This means 'not' in front of a verb.
e.g. Je **ne** vais **pas** en ville
      I am **not** going to town.

Nouns These are the names of things or people.
e.g. table, chair, boy, Marc, etc.

Objects
(a) Direct
The person or thing to which an action or feeling is directly transferred.
e.g. J'aime **l'école**.
      I like school.
      Nous voyons **les enfants**.
      We see the children.

(b) Indirect
The person or thing to which something is said or done.
e.g. Je parle **aux enfants**.
      I speak to the children.
      Je **leur** donne les devoirs.
      I give homework **to them**.

Past participle That part of each verb which is used with 'avoir' or 'être' to form the Perfect tense.
e.g. J'ai **donné**
      Je suis **allé**

Pronouns Words used instead of nouns but referring to them.
e.g. 'il'/'elle'/'nous'/etc.

Reflexive verbs Verbs which refer to actions done to oneself.
e.g. **se laver**   to wash (oneself)

Superlatives Expressions which mean 'most' or '-est'.
e.g. l'enfant le plus intelligent
      the most intelligent child
      la plus jolie ville
      the prettiest town

Tenses
(a) Present tense
Those parts of the verb which tell us about the present.
e.g. Je vais en ville.
      I am going to town.
(b) Perfect tense
One of the tenses which tells us what has happened in the past.
e.g. Je suis allé en ville.
      I went to town.

Vowels These are the letters 'a' 'e' 'i' 'o' 'u'.

Vocabulary

New words which appear in Volume 2 for the first time.

A

un **abricot**   apricot
Accès aux quais   to the platforms
acceuillir   to welcome
accompagner   to accompany
accoutumé   accustomed
J'accuse reception de . . .   I acknowledge receipt of . . .
une **adresse**   address
les **adultes**   adults
l'**aérobic**   aerobics
un **aéroport**   airport
les **affaires** (f)   belongings
une **affiche**   notice
un(e) **Africain(e)**   African
l'**Afrique** (f)   Africa
une **agence de voyages**   travel agent's
un **agent (de police)**   policeman
agréer   to agree
aider   to help
les **aires de jeux**   play areas
l'**alcool**   alcohol
l'**Allemagne** (f)   Germany
un(e) **Allemand(e)**   German
un **aller simple**   single ticket
un **aller et retour**   return ticket
allumer   to switch on
une **ambulance**   ambulance
amusant   amusing
s'**amuser**   to enjoy oneself
un **ananas**   pineapple
l'**Angleterre** (f)   England
un **annuaire**   telephone directory
un **appareil-photo**   camera
appeler   to call
appliquer   to apply
apprécier   to appreciate
s'**approcher de**   to approach
après   after
l'**architecture** (f)   architecture
un **arrêt d'autobus**   bus-stop
s'**arrêter**   to stop
l'**arrivée** (f)   arrival
arriver   to arrive
les **artichauts** (m)   artichokes
un **ascenseur**   lift
les **asperges** (f)   asparagus
assis   sitting

l'**assurance** (f)   insurance
Attention!   Look out!
faire **attention**   to pay attention
attraper   to catch
une **auberge**   inn
Au feu!   Fire!
Au voleur!   Stop thief!
un **autocar**   coach
l'**Autriche** (f)   Austria
avant de   before
l'**avertisseur** (m)   horn (car)
un **avion**   plane
un **avis**   advice/opinion

B

les **bagages** (m)   luggage
la **bague**   ring
se **baigner**   to bathe
une station **balnéaire**   seaside resort
la **bande dessinée**   cartoon
la **banlieue**   suburbs/outskirts
en **bas**   below/downstairs
bavarder   to chat
la **Belgique**   Belgium
faire des **bêtises**   to play the fool
besoin   need
bientôt   soon
le **bifteck**   steak
la **biologie**   biology
blessé   injured
blesser   to wound
la **blessure**   wound
un **bleu**   bruise
le **bloc sanitaire**   washrooms/toilets
la **boîte aux lettres**   letter-box
de **bonne heure**   early
au **bord de**   by the side of
le **Bottin**   telephone directory
la **bouche**   mouth
la **boum**   party
le **bras**   arm
bricoler   'Do-it-yourself'
(se) **brosser**   to brush
les **brûlures d'estomac**   indigestion
le **bureau d'acceuil**   reception (office)
le **bureau de renseignements**   information office
le **bureau de tabac**   tobacconist

C

une **cabine téléphonique**   telephone kiosk
le **cadeau**   present
le **cadran**   dial
la **caisse**   till/cash-desk
le **canard**   duck
la **cantine**   canteen
la **canne à pêche**   fishing-rod
le **capot**   bonnet (car)
car   for/because
un **car**   coach
la **carte**   map
la **ceinture de sécurité**   safety-belt
le **censeur**   Deputy-head (school)
la **chaise pliante**   folding-chair
chaque   each
un **chèque de voyage**   traveller's cheque
la **cheville**   ankle
les **cheveux** (*m*)   hair
la **chimie**   Chemistry
la **Chine**   China
le **choix**   choice
les **choux de Bruxelles**   Brussels sprouts
le **chou-fleur**   cauliflower
le **club des jeunes**   Youth Club
le **coffre**   boot (car)
le **coin**   corner
en **colère**   angry
une heure de **colle**   detention
collectionner   to collect
le **combiné**   receiver (telephone)
commander   to order
comment   how
la **compagnie d'assurance**   insurance company
comprendre   to understand
un **comprimé**   tablet
le **comptoir**   counter
conduire   to drive
le **confort**   comfort
(un jour de) **congé**   a day's holiday
connaître   to know
(les mieux) **connus**   the best known
conseiller   to advise
les **conserves**   preserves
la **consigne**   left-luggage office
construire   to build/make
consulter   to consult
continuer   to continue
la **contrebande**   contraband
le **contrôle des passeports**   passport control
la **Corse**   Corsica
à **côté de**   by the side of
la **Côte d'Azur**   the Mediterranean coast of France
la **côtelette**   chop
le **cou**   neck
se **coucher**   to lie down/go to bed
le **coude**   elbow
coudre   to sew

couler   to flow
un **coup de soleil**   sun-burn
un **coup de veine**   a windfall/stroke of luck
courir   to run
le **courrier**   mail
un **cours**   lesson
la **crème**   cream
la **crevaison**   puncture
une **crise de foie**   a stomach upset
les **crudités**   chopped raw salad

D

d'accord   agreed
le **Danemark**   Denmark
dangereux   dangerous
Danois   Danish
décider   to decide
déclarer   to declare
défense de . . .   it is forbidden to . . .
dehors   outside
délicieux   delicious
une **demi-heure**   half an hour
les **dents** (*f*)   teeth
le **départ**   departure
se **dépêcher**   to hurry
dépenser   to spend
dernier   last
descendre   to go down
désolé   very sorry
le **dessin**   drawing
le **dessin animé**   cartoon (animated)
devenir   to become
devoir   to have to/to owe
les **devoirs**   homework
d'habitude   usually
Mon **Dieu**   Good heavens
difficile   difficult
la **difficulté**   difficulty
le **disque**   record
distrait   absent-minded
le **doigt**   finger
le **dos**   back
la **douane**   the Customs
le **douanier**   the customs' officer

E

l'**Écosse**   Scotland
écouter   to listen to
s'**écrier**   to shout
écrire   to write
une **écurie**   stable

l'**embrayage** (*m*)   clutch
un **emplacement**   pitch
un **emploi de temps**   timetable
une(e) **employé(e)**   assistant
enchanté   delighted
ennuyant   annoying
ennuyeux   boring
enrhumé   (to) have a cold
entendre   to hear
entre   between
(bien)-**entretenu**   well-kept
les **environs**   the surrounding area
envoyer   to send
une **épaule**   shoulder
l'**Espagne**   Spain
espérer   to hope
les **épinards**   spinach
un **essuie-glace**   windscreen-wiper
une **étable**   cowshed
un **étage**   story (house)
les **Etats-Unis**   United States
un **étranger**   stranger/foreigner
à l'**étranger**   abroad
étudier   to study
les **événements** (*mpl*)   events
exactement   exactly
un **examen**   exam
par **exemple**   for example
expliquer   to explain

F

facile   easy
facilement   easily
faciliter   to ease
le **facteur**   postman
faire la fête   to have a good time
faire mal à   to hurt
faire son piano   to do one's piano practise
il **faut**   it is necessary
favori   favourite
la **fente**   slot
fermer   to close
fêter   to celebrate
le **feu clignotant**   car indicator light
le **feu de position**   side-light
les **feux**   traffic-lights
la **fiche**   form
la **fièvre**   high temperature
la **figure**   face
(regarder) **fixement**   to stare
la **framboise**   raspberry
les **freins** (*mpl*)   brakes
les **frites** (*fpl*)   chips
le **front**   forehead
fumer   to smoke

G

gagner   to earn
Gallois   Welsh
la **gare routière**   the bus station
le **genou**   knee
gentil   nice/kind
la **géographie**   geography
un **gigot d'agneau**   leg of lamb
la **gorge**   throat
la **Grande-Bretagne**   Great Britain
grave   serious
la **grève**   strike
la **grippe**   'flu
le **guichet**   counter/booking-office
la **gymnastique**   gymnastics

H

s'**habiller**   to get dressed
les **haricots**   beans
herbeux   grassy
à l'**heure**   on time
heureusement   happily
hier   yesterday
une **histoire**   story

I

les **Îles Baléares**   the Balearic Islands
imprimé   printed (matter)
inconnu   unknown/a stranger
l'**Inde**   India
indiquer   to point out
une **infirmière**   nurse
inquiet   anxious
s'**inquiéter**   to be worried
l'**instruction civique**   Civics
l'**instruction religieuse**   RE
interdit   forbidden
intéressant   interesting
s'**intéresser à**   to be interested in
interroger   to question
l'**Irlande**   Ireland
l'**Italie**   Italy

J

la **jambe**   leg
le **Japon**   Japan
le **jardinage**   gardening
jeter   to throw
un **jeton**   disc
jeune   young

la **joue**   cheek
jouer à cache-cache   to play hide-and-seek
jouer un tour à   to play a trick on
le **jour férié**   bank holiday
un **journal** (*pl.* **journaux**)   newspaper(s)
la **journée**   day
jusqu'à   until/as far as

K

la **kermesse**   village fair/fête
le **kiosque**   kiosk

L

laisser   to leave
la **langue**   tongue
les **lavabos**   washrooms
se **laver**   to get washed
la **lecture**   reading
leur   their/to them
la **levée**   collection
se **lever**   to get up
la **lèvre**   lip
libre   free
libre-service   self-service
le **lieu**   place
la **ligne**   line
la **liste**   list
la **livre**   pound
la **location**   hiring
Londres   London
le **long de**   along
louer   to hire

M

la **main**   hand
mal   badly
la **maladie**   illness
malheureusement   unfortunately
manquer   to miss
la **maquette**   small model
marcher   to walk
la **marque**   make
la **matière**   subject
le **mécanicien**   mechanic
meilleur   better/best (adjective)
même   same
le **menton**   chin
la **femme de ménage**   maid
le **métro**   underground railway
mettre   to put

se **mettre à**   to begin
se **mettre en colère**   to get angry
mieux   better/best (adverb)
mille   thousand
le **monde**   world
monter   to go up
montrer   to show
la **montre**   wrist-watch
le **mot**   word
le **moteur**   engine
multiple   many
le **musée**   museum
la **musique**   music

N

la **natation**   swimming
naturellement   naturally
néanmoins   nevertheless
nécessaire   necessary
le **neveu**   nephew
le **nez**   nose
ni   nor
la **nièce**   niece
le **niveau**   level
le **nom**   name
non plus   neither
nous-mêmes   ourselves
les **nouvelles** (*fpl*)   news
la **Nouvelle-Zélande**   New Zealand

O

un **objet de valeur**   a valuable object
obligé   compelled
occidental   western
une **oie**   goose
ombragé   shaded
un **oeil**   eye
offert   offered/given
l'**or**   gold
une **ordonnance**   prescription
une **oreille**   ear
l'**orteil** (*m*)   toe
ou   or
ouvrir   to open

P

les **Palais du Parlement**   Houses of Parliament
en **panne**   broken down
les **pantoufles** (*fpl*)   slippers

la **papeterie** stationer's
le **parfum** perfume
parler to speak
parce que because
le **pare-brise** windscreen
le **pare-chocs** bumper
les **parents** parents/relatives
parmi amongst
par terre on the ground
partir to leave
partout everywhere
le **passage clouté** pedestrian crossing
passer to pass/spend/take (of an exam)
le **passe-port** passport
les **pâtisseries** (*fpl*) pastries
patiner to skate
les **Pays-Bas** the Netherlands
le **Pays de Galles** Wales
pendant during
pendant que whilst
penser to think
perdre to lose
(une heure de) **perme** a free lesson
le **permis de conduire** driving-licence
le **petit déjeuner** breakfast
les **petits-enfants** grandchildren
les **petits pois** peas
à **peu près** approximately
la **phare** headlight
la **physique** physics
la **pièce de théâtre** play
le **pied** foot
le **piéton** pedestrian
une **pièce de monnaie** coin
le **plaisir** pleasure
en **plein air** in the open air
(faire) le **plein d'essence** to fill up with petrol
pleurer to cry
le **pneu** tyre
le **poignet** wrist
le **poisson d'avril** April fool
la **poitrine** chest
le **policier** policeman
les **pommes à l'anglaise** boiled potatoes
les **pommes de terre** potatoes
les **pompiers** firemen
la **pompe** pump
le **pompiste** pump-attendant
populaire popular
la **porcherie** pigsty
le **portefeuille** wallet
le **porte-monnaie** purse
la **portière** door (car/train)
poser des questions to ask questions
un **poste de police** police-station
le **potage** soup
les **poubelles** (*fpl*) dustbins
le **pouce** thumb

le **poulailler** hen-house
pouvoir to be able
préféré favourite
prendre to take
préparer to prepare
présenter to present/introduce
prier to beg
prochain next
profiter de to take advantage of
propre own/clean
le **propriétaire** proprietor
les **provisions** (*fpl*) groceries

Q

le **quai** quay/plafform
le **quartier** district
quel which
quelqu'un someone
quelque chose something
le **quotidien** daily paper

R

le **radiateur** radiator
les **radis** radishes
ramasser to pick up
ranger to tidy away
se **rappeler** to remember
la **raquette** racket
rarement rarely
recevoir to receive
le **réchaud** stove (camping)
reconnaissant grateful
redoubler to repeat
remarquer to notice
le **récepteur** receiver
les **renseignements** thanks
rentrer to go back/return
renverser to knock over
le **repas** meal
la **réponse** reply
réserver to reserve
le **réservoir à essence** petrol-tank
en **retard** late
retenir to book
le **rétroviseur** driving-mirror
retourner to return
le **réveil** alarm clock
se **réveiller** to wake up
revenir to come back
la **revue** magazine
ne . . . **rien** nothing
rire to laugh

les **rognons** (mpl)   kidneys
le **rond-point**   roundabout
rôti   roast
la **roue de secours**   spare wheel
la **routine journalière**   daily routine
la **Russie**   Russia

S

la **sac à dos**   rucksack
le **sac à main**   handbag
le **sac de couchage**   sleeping-bag
sale   dirty
la **salle d'attente**   waiting-room
sans   without
la **santé**   health
la **Sardaigne**   Sardinia
sauvage   wild
le **savon**   soap
la **semaine**   week
le **séjour**   stay
le **sel**   salt
seulement   only
le **siège**   seat
les **sciences naturelles**   Natural Science
sixième   sixth
soi   oneself
le **soin**   care
SNCF   French railways
soigner   to look after
la **soirée**   evening (party)
la **sorte**   sort
sortir   to go out
souffrant   unwell
souffrir   to suffer
le **souper**   evening meal
la **spécialité**   speciality
le **spectacle**   show
la **station balnéaire**   resort
stationner   to park
la **Suisse**   Switzerland
supporter   to support/bear
surtout   especially
un **surveillant**   supervisor

T

la **table pliante**   folding table
la **tante**   aunt
taquiner   to tease
tarif réduit   reduced rate

téléphoner   to telephone
tellement   so
le **terrain de camping**   campsite
la **tête**   head
le **timbre-poste**   postage stamp
tomber   to fall
la **tonalité**   dialling tone
toucher un chèque   to cash a cheque
se **tourner**   to turn round
tout de suite   straightaway
le **travail**   work
un **travail de recherches**   project
travailler   to work
la **tranquillité**   tranquillity
les **travaux manuels/pratiques**   craft
se **tromper**   to make a mistake
le **trottoir**   path
trouver   to find
se **trouver**   to be found

U

utile   useful

V

les **vacances** (*fpl*)   holidays
la **valise**   suitcase
la **vallée**   valley
le **veau**   veal
venir   to come
le **ventre**   stomach
vérifier   to check
le **visage**   face
la **voie**   track
le(la) **voisin(e)**   neighbour
le **volant**   steering-wheel
voler   to steal
Au **voleur!**   Stop thief!
vouloir   to wish/want
le **voyage**   journey
voyager   to travel
le **voyageur**   traveller
vraiment   really

Y

les **yeux** (*mpl*)   eyes

Index